THE LUCENT LIBRARY OF CONFLICT IN THE MIDDLE EAST

Human Rights in the Middle East

Human Rights in the Middle East

Other books in The Lucent Library of Conflict in the Middle East series include:

The Arab-Israeli Conflict
The Middle East: An Overview
The Palestinians
U.S. Involvement in the Middle East: Inciting Conflict

THE LUCENT LIBRARY OF CONFLICT IN THE MIDDLE EAST

Human Rights in the Middle East

By Gail B. Stewart

LUCENT BOOKS

An imprint of Thomson Gale, a part of The Thomson Corporation

Detroit • New York • San Francisco • San Diego • New Haven, Conn. • Waterville, Maine • London • Munich

Lauri Friedman, Series Editor

For more information, contact
Lucent Books
27500 Drake Rd.
Farmington Hills, MI 48331-3535
Or you can visit our Internet site at http://www.gale.com

LIBRARY OF CONGRESS CATALOGING-IN-PUBLICATION DATA

Stewart, Gail B., 1949–
     Human rights in the Middle East / by Gail B. Stewart.
        p. cm. — (Lucent library of conflict in the Middle East)
     Includes bibliographical reference and index.
     ISBN 1-59018-488-2 (hardcover : alk. paper)
     1. Human rights—Middle East—Juvenile literature. I. Title. II. Series.
     JC599.M628S84 2004
     323'.044'0956—dc22
                                                                    2004010836

Printed in the United States of America

CONTENTS

FOREWORD

On May 29, 2004, a group of Islamic terrorists attacked a housing compound in Khobar, Saudi Arabia, where hundreds of petroleum industry employees, many of them Westerners, lived. The terrorists ran through the complex, taking hostages and murdering people they considered infidels. At one point, they came across an Iraqi-American engineer who was Muslim. As the helpless stranger stood frozen before them, the terrorists debated whether or not he deserved to die. "He's an American, we should shoot him," said one of the terrorists. "We don't shoot Muslims," responded another. The militants calmly discussed the predicament for several minutes and finally came to an agreement. "We are not going to shoot you," they told the terrorized man. After preaching to him about the righteousness of Islam, they continued their bloody spree.

The engineer's life was spared because the terrorists decided that his identity as a Muslim overrode all other factors that marked him as their enemy. Among the unfortunate twenty-two others killed that day were Swedes, Americans, Indians, and Filipinos whose identity as foreigners or Westerners or, as the terrorists proclaimed, "Zionists and crusaders," determined their fate. Although the Muslim engineer whose life was spared had far more in common with his murdered coworkers than with the terrorists, in the militants' eyes he was on their side.

The terrorist attacks in Khobar typify the conflict in the Middle East today, where fighting is often done along factionalist lines. Indeed, historically the peoples of the Middle East have been unified not by national identity but by intense loyalty to a tribe, ethnic group, and above all, religious sect. For example, Iraq is home to Sunni Muslims, Shiite Muslims, Kurds, Turkomans, and Christian Assyrians who identify themselves by ethnic and religious affiliation first, and as Iraqis second. When conflict erupts, ancient, sometimes obscure alliances determine whom they fight with and whom they fight against. Navigating this complex labyrinth of loyalties is key to understanding conflict in the Middle East, because these identities generate not only passionate allegiance to one's own group but also fanatic intolerance and fierce hatred of others.

Russian author Anton Chekhov once astutely noted, "Love, friendship, respect do not unite people as much as a common hatred for something." His words serve as a slogan for conflict in the Middle East, where religious belief and tribal allegiances perpetuate strong codes of honor and revenge, and hate is used to motivate people to join in a common cause. The methods of generating hatred in the Middle East are pervasive and overt. After Friday noon prayers, for example, imams in both Sunni and Shiite mosques deliver fiery sermons that inflame tensions between the sects that run high in nearly every Muslim country where the two groups coexist. With similar intent to incite hatred, Iranian satellite television programs broadcast forceful messages to Shiite Muslims across the Middle East, condemning certain groups as threats to Shiite values.

Perhaps some of the most astounding examples of people bonding in hatred are found in the Israeli-Palestinian conflict. In the Palestinian territories, men, women, and children are consistently taught to hate Israel, and even to die in the fight for Palestine. In spring 2004, the terrorist group Hamas went so far as to launch an online children's magazine that demonizes Israel and encourages youths to become suicide bombers. On the other hand, some sectors of Israeli society work hard to stereotype and degrade Palestinians in order to harden Israelis against the Palestinian cause. Is-

raeli journalist Barry Chamish, for example, dehumanizes Palestinians when he writes, "The Palestinians know nothing of the creation of beauty, engage in no serious scholarship, pass nothing of greatness down the ages. Their legacy is purely of destruction."

This type of propaganda inflames tensions in the Middle East, leading to a cycle of violence that has thus far proven impossible to break. Terrorist organizations send suicide bombers into Israeli cities to retaliate for Israeli assassinations of Palestinian leaders. The Israeli military, in response, leads incursions into Palestinian villages to demolish blocks upon blocks of homes, shops, and schools, further impoverishing an already desperate community. To avenge the destruction and death left in the wake of the incursions, Palestinians recruit more suicide bombers to launch themselves at civilian targets in Israeli cities. Neither side is willing to let a violent attack go unreciprocated, undermining nonviolent attempts to mediate the conflict, and the vicious cycle continues.

The books in the Lucent Library of Conflict in the Middle East help readers understand this embattled region of the world. Annotated bibliographies provide readers with ideas for further research, while fully documented primary and secondary source quotations enhance the text. Each book in the series explores a different facet of conflict in the Middle East; together they provide students with a wealth of information as well as launching points for further study and discussion.

A More Secret Problem

In January 1947, just two years after the end of World War II, the United Nations held a special session. Its purpose was to draft a declaration of rights that it believed applied to every man, woman, and child on earth. The task was difficult, for the representatives of the various nations often disagreed over what rights could truly be called "human rights." Neverthless, on December 10, 1948, the world's first declaration on human rights was ratified.

Although the declaration was groundbreaking in its scope, there was no power of law behind it. Nations could continue to allow human rights violations without being penalized. However, the declaration was important for the goals it set down. The freedoms it listed—though not in place in all nations—were a reminder of what each nation on earth could strive to become.

A Difficult Region

International human rights groups such as Amnesty International and Human Rights Watch have noted that the Middle East is a region of the world that has often had difficulty instituting human rights for its citizens. In some cases, human rights are violated because of strict religious fundamentalism. In other cases, long-standing hostility between cultural or religious groups leads to violations of rights. Sometimes rights are suspended because of war or because of an especially dictatorial leader.

Whatever the cause, a number of nations in the Middle East have been criticized for not adhering to the Universal Declaration of Human Rights. From the use of torture on prisoners and the supression of art and expression to the forced labor of children and the lack of voting rights for women, too many

Prisoners executed by Afghanistan's Taliban hang in a Kabul square. Rigid religious fundamentalism led the Taliban to commit a number of extreme human rights abuses.

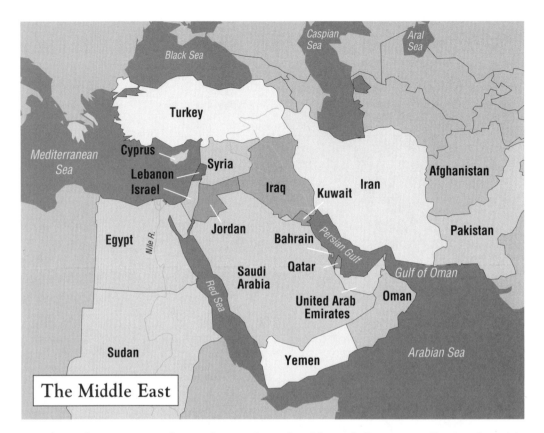

The Middle East

people in that region are being deprived of freedoms to which they are entitled.

In recent times, much attention has been focused on the Middle East. The U.S.-led invasion of Iraq and the escalating violence between Palestine and Israel have concerned people around the world. And since the terrorist attacks on the United States on September 11, 2001, the region's close association with international terrorism has been a source of widely publicized concern. Yet the wide abuse of human rights, though perhaps done more quietly behind the closed doors of government, is just as deadly to many who live in that part of the world.

CHAPTER 1

Systems of Injustice

According to human rights experts, a government's true commitment to protecting its citizens can be seen in the way it treats those suspected of criminal activity. One human rights worker explains what he looks for to determine whether prisoners' rights are being violated:

> We look for evidence that a suspect is informed of the charges against him or her, and if the person is given an open trial where they're allowed to defend themselves. Even more important, we want to see that every suspect, every prisoner is treated humanely while in custody. That means no withholding of meals, no beatings or forced confessions, no executions.[1]

Throughout the Middle East, a number of governments fail to protect even these basic human rights of individuals suspected of crimes.

From Shah to Sharia

One of the nations frequently criticized by human rights groups is Iran, one of the largest countries in the Middle East. For many years, Iran was a monarchy headed by a king, or shah. Under this system, there were many human rights violations committed against Iran's people, especially under the last shah, Mohammad Reza Pahlavi.

In 1979 a revolution took place that changed Iran's system of government to a theocracy, or rule by the clergy. In this case, it was a fundamentalist Muslim, the Ayatollah Ruhollah Khomeini, who replaced the shah. Instead of operating under the legal system used by the shah's government, Iran wrote a new legal code based on sharia, the body of Islamic law. The rules and guidelines set

After taking control of Iran in 1979, the Ayatollah Khomeini implemented a repressive government based on a conservative interpretation of Islamic law.

down by sharia are taken from the Koran (the Islamic holy book) as well as the sunna, the traditional teachings of the prophet Muhammad.

Because Khomeini and his associates were fundamentalist Muslims, their interpretation of sharia was very conservative. As a result, they legally changed punishments to reflect a harsher style of justice. A thief would have his right hand cut off, for instance, and a highway robber would have his right hand and left foot cut off. Anyone convicted of adultery could be stoned to death.

Such punishments were viewed by most of the world as medieval. International human rights groups were very vocal in their protests, but Khomeini's reply was simple: Their justice system reflected Iran's religious beliefs, and it was no one's business but Iran's how that religion was interpreted.

Little Has Changed

Ironically, even though one of the reasons that people had been dissatisfied with the shah was because of his human rights record, the new government has had a far worse record of abusing the rights of its citizens. In its first two years,

757 people—most of them former supporters of the shah—were executed by firing squads. Thousands of others were jailed after being arrested for vaguely stated crimes such as "sowing corruption on earth," a phrase from sharia that could mean a number of things, from lying to a police officer to criticizing the new government.

Not surprisingly, the harshness of the new leadership angered many Iranians. High school and university students staged protests against the government, but the fundamentalists clamped down harder. A former inmate of Evin, Iran's largest prison, said later that the government wanted to punish them for their political views and at the same time demonstrate how futile it was for them to protest. "The regime had one overriding aim from the moment it arrested us," he says. "It was to force us to reject our beliefs, and show that its lashes were stronger than our ideals."[2]

Although the Ayatollah Khomeini died in 1989, Iran's fundamentalist Islamic government has continued to violate the rights of those suspected of crimes. Some Iranians believe that their country will never be a proponent of human rights, simply because of the way the government is set up. Iran has a reform-minded president, but the judicial branch of government is controlled by very conservative religious

In 1979 an Iranian firing squad executes Kurds convicted of treason. Khomeini's government executed hundreds of people during its first two years.

leaders who have regularly vetoed every new program the president suggests.

The sharia continues to be the backbone of Iran's judicial system. In addition to regular police officers, vigilante groups of religious police patrol the cities, watching for violations such as drinking alcohol or coed dancing—both taboo in Iran. Trials for the accused are almost always secret, and no defendant is allowed a defense lawyer. In fact, the very idea of a defense attorney is considered "a Western absurdity."[3] People in Iran can be arrested and jailed without knowing why, and are frequently held for several weeks before being allowed to phone their families to explain their whereabouts.

When a prisoner is finally permitted a visitor, prison guards make sure that there is no discussion about the case or the circumstances of the arrest. One man recalled how difficult such constraints were when he was in prison: "During visits, I was not allowed to say more than a few words, such as greetings, and how are you and I am well. During telephone conversations, too, there was always someone standing next to me and telling me directly that I was only allowed to say those few things."[4]

Guilty

Trials in Iran are not held until a prisoner has confessed. Experts claim that that explains why torture is so impor-

"The Person Who Enters Is Lost"

In the following excerpt from a 2001 article titled "Syria: Time to Break with Legacy of Torture and Dehumanization," the Middle East Online *presents a depressing portrait of Syria's Tadmur Military Prison, in which human rights abuses abound.*

In a report [of Tadmur prison] . . . Amnesty International paints a grim picture of an anachronistic penitentiary institution so notorious for its culture of dehumanizing torture and ill-treatment that it is referred to in Syria as the place where "the person who enters is lost and the one who leaves is born."

Among the thousands detained over the years, many have frequently been tortured while held in total isolation from the outside world for months or years without charge or trial. Many thousands of families have been kept in the dark about the fate of their relatives. Some, whose loved ones "disappeared" after arrest, fear the worst. . . .

Torture is so routine that detainees are commonly tortured as soon as they arrive in Tadmur, in what is known as the *"haflat al-istiqbal"* or, "reception party." A former detainee held between 1996 and 1999 gave this account of a "reception" at Tadmur: "I was forced into the tyre [tire] and ordered to place my hands between my legs; my feet were then stretched and painfully tied with a strong rope to an iron bar to prevent me from moving them in any direction. After that they took the blindfold off my eyes and the lashing started. Two guards were whipping me at the same time. . . . Amidst our cries of pain we began to count the lashes: one, two . . . ten, twenty, thirty . . . then one loses count and concentration."

tant to the system. "Under the bizarre justice system of the Islamic Republic," writes one critic, "convictions of the accused are primarily based not on evidence, but on confessions. Thus the use of torture as a tool to obtain confession is built into the very structure of the . . . order."[5]

Ghollam Nibkin, an Iranian American who had converted to the Mormon faith while living in the United States, was arrested in Iran in 1996 by religious police. He was whipped with electric cable on the bare soles of his feet, flogged with a leather whip, and hung upside down during interrogations. He finally confessed that he had indeed converted, and only after his family bribed officials was he saved from execution. Instead, Nibkin was transferred to a mental hospital, where he was kept for several months and forcibly injected with drugs.

The violence associated with Iran's judicial system frightens its citizens, but few are willing to risk a possible jail sentence by openly criticizing the government. One man who did offer criticism was journalist Mohammad Hajizadeh. Hajizadeh strongly supported the candidacy of Mohammad Khatami, who was elected president of Iran in 1997. In a 2003 open letter to Khatami, Hajizadeh questioned the harsh power of the conservative clerics.

He pointed out that the 1979 revolution had occurred in part as a reaction to the human rights violations of the shah. "Some twenty-odd years ago," he wrote, "we broke the doors of the prisons. . . . We were supposed to transform the shah's prisons into cultural centers and libraries." Instead, he said, the prisons have become even more crowded with people whose rights have diminished under the fundamentalist government. All are presumed guilty under the current system, and none are allowed to defend themselves. "Is it really correct," asked Hajizadeh, "to send everyone to prison over every matter? . . . What if, as a journalist, I go to the same prison on charges of writing something as the smuggler of a ton of narcotics, as the man who has not paid alimony to his wife, and so forth?"[6]

Reason for Hope?

Even though Iran's human rights record has been poor, some feel a sense of optimism that Iran's justice system may begin to improve. The stumbling block for change has been the conservative clerics in the government who oppose the reforms brought up by the president and other elected officials. However, there has been division among the clerics themselves about the direction Iran is heading.

In the publication *Human Rights Watch World Report 2003*, the group's advocates note that one cleric resigned because he felt that the government was becoming too repressive: "In his widely circulated letter of resignation, the [cleric] . . . acccused Iran's clerical leaders of directing and encouraging 'a bunch of club wielders' and of 'marrying the ill-tempered, ugly hag of violence to religion.'"[7] If other clerics feel the same, say human rights workers, there may be more room for cooperation on justice issues between the elected officials and the religious leaders.

Torture in Saudi Arabia

Another nation that has been much criticized by human rights agencies in recent years is Saudi Arabia—and for many of the same reasons. The executive director of Amnesty International, William F. Schulz, announced that Saudi Arabia "has gotten away with arbitrary detention and torture for years, while escaping international scrutiny."[8]

In Saudi Arabia, violence toward people suspected of a crime sometimes begins even before they are taken to jail. Human rights workers from Amnesty International interviewed a young woman who had firsthand experience with such treatment. She tells of her arrest by the religious police, or *mutawa'een*, who suspected her of possessing alcohol:

> Three *mutawa'een* burst into my home and one of them grabbed me by my hair and pulled me with such force that I heard every ligament in my head click. . . . I had glasses on. . . . One of [the *mutawa'een*] grabbed my glasses off my head and spat in my face. . . . He was dragging me down the stairs, stamped on my glasses, and took me out to the car.[9]

Once suspects are in custody, police or prison guards often try to get them to confess, for that will mean a speedy trial. As the president of Saudi Arabia's administrative court explains, "Confes-

sion is the highest form of evidence that can be used to convict a defendant."[10]

The Saudi justice system's strong reliance on confession, say observers, has led to abuses. Often prisoners are beaten to extract an admission of guilt. One young prisoner was forced to stand in his cell for nine days in a row, chained to a gate with his hands above his head. Guards beat him with ax handles until he finally confessed. "It went on and on," he recalls. "I used to consider myself a strong person, but everybody has their breaking point. I was alone and in pain, and if it wasn't me being beaten, it was others, and I could hear their screams."[11]

Many times, guards get a confession based on false promises. Amnesty International workers interviewed a young man who had been accused of stealing a briefcase. He had managed to endure being beaten and kicked with steel-toed boots for days. Finally, he says, a guard explained that if he confessed to the crime, all charges against him would almost certainly be dropped. So, "I said I took the briefcase, which was a lie," he says. When he appeared before the judge, he realized that his confession had sealed his conviction. "I told the judge that I confessed only to stop the torture," he explains. "I showed the judge the marks of torture. The judge didn't even seem to listen."[12] The young prisoner was sentenced to a year in prison and 240 lashes for a crime that he maintains he did not commit.

Extreme Punishment

Whipping or flogging is allowed in the Saudi constitution. According to a num-

"Everyone Is Tired of These Things"

The Taliban's brand of justice in Afghanistan shocked human rights workers throughout the world. In this excerpt from a June 1998 article from the Japan Times, *the Taliban's use of amputation is explained.*

Four Afghan doctors, their faces hidden behind surgical masks, amputated the right hand and left foot of a convicted thief Friday before a crowd of about 2,000 people.

The thief, Bashir Ahmed, was a soldier in the Taliban religious army when he robbed three people of $500 near the front line in northeastern Afghanistan, said an unidentified religious scholar who oversaw the amputation.

The Taliban religious army, which rules 85 percent of Afghanistan, including the capital of Kabul, has imposed a strict brand of Islamic justice in its territory. It calls for the amputation of limbs of convicted thieves, execution of murderers, and the public beating of criminals convicted of lesser crimes, including women who do not wear the required covering from head to toe.

Outside the sports stadium where the amputation took place, dozens of boys played soccer. Asked why he wasn't watching the amputation, Abdul Jamil said, "Everyone is tired of these things." . . .

The Taliban army almost weekly holds public punishments in its sports stadium.

The Taliban amputated this man's hand as punishment for theft.

ber of former prisoners interviewed by human rights workers, most of the lashes they received were administered in a special "whipping area." Guards use a specially made whip that is nearly four feet long. A heavy piece of lead is attached to the tip, which not only breaks the skin but can cause internal damage to muscles and bones. One man says that after a few lashes he was almost unconscious, but "the guard would raise me up to continue the whipping. I was amazed to find myself still alive after the seventieth lash. My back was bleeding . . . [and] I cried."[13]

The most lashes ever handed down as punishment is four thousand, which were administered to a man accused of robbery. He was given about fifty lashes every two weeks—just long enough for the bloody welts to begin healing before they were opened with the whip again.

Not surprisingly, some prisoners die in custody—either from torture or from the lashes they receive as punishment. The lacerations frequently become infected, and prisoners rarely receive medical care. In 1996 a twenty-one-year-old man died from kidney failure after being struck repeatedly with the whip and an ax handle.

Former Saudi Arabian king Abd al-Aziz punished lawbreakers with beheading, a practice that continues today.

While torture and lashing are condemned by human rights organizations throughout the world, it is Saudi Arabia's wide use of the death penalty that causes the most concern. The execution method used by the Saudi government, known as "death by the blade," has been practiced for hundreds of years.

As recently as fifty years ago, mass beheadings of large groups of people were conducted at the order of the king to make a statement of force. A British journalist recently spoke with a man who had flown over the Saudi desert with King Abd al-Aziz, who ruled the country until his death in 1953. The king, said the man, wanted to show him a village:

> I didn't know why, but when we got overhead, it was just a deserted place with a few stray dogs. And then the king said to me: "The people of this village used to rob the caravans to Mecca, and I warned them to stop. They didn't listen to me, so I warned them again. Again, they didn't listen. So I sent my guards to the village and they cut off the heads of every man, woman, and child. And they waited for villagers to return from far away. And they cut off their heads, too. And there was no more robbery. If you are going to rule, you must use your power and be firm."[14]

The nation's reliance on beheadings continues today. In fact, Saudi Arabia has one of the highest yearly execution rates of any nation on earth. Amnesty International has recorded 1,409 executions between 1980 and 2002, but human rights experts in the Middle East maintain that the number could be much higher, since some executions occur behind prison walls and details are not made public.

Unlike in some nations that reserve the death penalty for the most heinous of crimes, such as murder, Saudi courts sentence prisoners to death for several nonviolent crimes. Witchcraft, drug dealing, and possession of alcohol are punishable by death, as are adultery and apostasy, or abandoning Islam.

Friday Afternoons

Beheadings in every district of Saudi Arabia are scheduled on Friday afternoons, after prayers. The prisoners are taken to the public square, blindfolded, and forced to kneel. Then the executioner brings his sharp sword down on the prisoner's neck. Saudis who have witnessed executions say that it often takes two or three strokes to completely sever the head.

Some human rights groups, unable to convince the Saudi government that beheadings are cruel, have asked that prisoners at least receive tranquilizers beforehand. However, people who have served time in Saudi prisons informed Human Rights Watch workers that they had not heard of any prisoners who were medicated before their execution.

One cell mate of a condemned man says that the anxiety and anguish of those sentenced to death is made more cruel because they are not told until the last minute whether that Friday is their execution day. "[My cell mate] is in a frenzy every Thursday afternoon, Friday morning in anticipation of execution," he says. "All his family have been told that he is already executed. But he is still inside."[15]

Crucifixion

The death penalty in Saudi Arabia is not limited to Saudi criminals. In fact, more foreign prisoners in Saudi prisons are executed than are Saudi citizens. A Scot named Sandy Mitchell, who says he was wrongly accused of setting off a car bomb in 2000, was held in solitary confinement for fifteen months before being allowed to see a lawyer. He was tortured into confessing.

Once he was able to confer with a lawyer, Mitchell was told that he would be executed by a method known as *al-hadd*, or "the limit," since it was a punishment reserved for the most heinous crimes. According to his lawyer, the sentence called for his head to be partially severed and his body affixed to an X-shaped cross in public view for a period of three days.

Only after the British government intervened was Mitchell spared. Mitchell said after the ordeal that he knew that he could be crucified at any time, and tried to find a way to deal with his fear. "I used to think, you can take my head," he said, "but you can't take my soul."[16]

Torture Under Saddam

Not all the human rights violations of prisoners occur in nations with fundamentalist Muslim leaders. In fact, some of the worst abuse occurred in Iraq, which until 2003 was controlled by the iron fist of its leader, Saddam Hussein. Saddam frequently quoted the Soviet dictator Joseph Stalin, who argued that to remain powerful, it was necessary to kill political opponents. "If there is a person," Stalin once said, "then there is a problem; if there is no person, then there is no problem."[17]

Nervous about political threats to his absolute power, Saddam made sure there was "no person" by carrying out massive purges of rival political parties. Anyone who was suspected of belonging to a party other than Saddam's Baath Party was jailed. Political prisoners were often tortured in an effort to get names of other people who were critical of Saddam and his administration. Though officially torture had been banned by the Iraqi constitution, the regime boasted 107 methods of torturing its enemies, including hair pulling, bastinado (beating the soles of the feet with a stick), electric shock, and the twisting of limbs until they broke. Sometimes family members were raped or tortured as a way of gaining the cooperation of a jailed political prisoner.

Many of the torture sessions were handled by Saddam himself, especially early in his regime. One political prisoner who underwent torture during this time describes the incredible pain that he suffered: "My arms and legs were tied together and I was hung by my feet from the ceiling. Saddam had converted a fan to take the weight of a man's body. As I was spun around, he beat me with

During his rule in Iraq, Saddam Hussein tortured and executed countless numbers of political enemies and criminals.

a length of rubber hose filled with rubble [small stones]."[18]

Saddam believed that it was crucial for people to know that the Iraqi government would not tolerate even the slightest criticism, and that it would be ruthless against those who dissented. For that reason, most political prisoners were executed once they had no further information to offer him.

Democratic Executions

In Saddam's Iraq, there were a total of twenty-four offenses that carried the death penalty. In addition to the crimes of murder and rape, capital offenses included arson, armed robbery, and homosexuality. Political crimes were vaguely stated; there were ten offenses that came under the heading of crimes against state security. These could include everything from a citizen's talking about the economy or government (both were categorized as "secret") to conversing with a foreign reporter.

Firing squad was the usual method of administering the death penalty, although Saddam created a special

Executions in Iraqi Prisons

In a 2001 article for the Middle East News *titled "Doctor Reveals Mass Slaughter at Saddam's Largest Jail," Iraqi doctor Maher Fakher Khashan gives chilling details of life (and death) in Iraq's most notorious prison, Abu Ghraib. During part of Saddam Hussein's regime, Khashan worked as head doctor of the prison.*

Khashan, who has fled Iraq to Jordan . . . was a witness to the 1998 massacre in which 2,000 inmates were executed in a single day as part of Saddam's so-called "prison cleansing campaign."

"Executions occur periodically at Abu Ghraib," [says Dr. Khashan]. "Every Wednesday some inmates are killed. A prisoner who is to be executed carries a number on his chest without a name." . . .

The entrance of special vehicles with iron boxes into Abu Ghraib grounds was a sign that executions were imminent. "These vehicles entered execution chambers and carried the corpses away. They bore the sign of 'mobile workshop' as a disguise," Khashan said. . . .

Abu Ghraib was overcrowded with approximately 10,000 inmates crammed into wards originally designed to accommodate 1,250 prisoners. "Inmates sleep on corridors. The price of a bed has surged to 50,000 dinars (approximately 30 U.S. dollars) per night," he said. . . .

Torture is routine in Abu Ghraib. Khashan said a special team of eye doctors is charged by Saddam to gouge out eyes of those executed inside the prison hospital.

The remains of an inmate executed at Abu Ghraib prison are exhumed.

method—"democratic execution"—for those convicted of political crimes. Instead of military marksmen shooting at the victims, Saddam required loyal Baath Party members to shoot political prisoners with handguns he provided. In his book *Saddam: King of Terror*, author Con Coughlin describes a video of a mass democratic execution that was held just days after Saddam took office:

The camera shows the [22] condemned men kneeling with blindfolds over their eyes, their wrists tied behind their backs. The camera then closes in showing a hand holding a gun, which fires a shot into the temple. The victims jerk and then crumple over. . . . In some instances the shootings prove inaccurate, leaving the victims still alive.[19]

The system of democratic execution was a way for Saddam to ensure the loyalty of his fellow Baathists, for it was a reminder of how swiftly and brutally death was dealt to enemies of the state.

Human Rights and War

Sometimes human rights of prisoners are violated because a nation is at war. In Israel, for example, where Palestinian suicide bombers have added to tensions in recent years, Israeli soldiers have been harshly criticized for their treatment of Palestinian civilians at a detention camp. In fact, four Israeli human rights groups accused soldiers of committing acts of torture on a number of occasions. Some prisoners have been dragged around by their hair, some have been slammed into walls while in handcuffs, and others have had their toes systematically broken during questioning.

Some army representatives have scoffed at the allegations of torture, saying that normal justice does not apply when such terrorism is occurring on an almost daily basis. "The army is subject to unprecedented conditions," said one government lawyer, "that make it impossible for us to work according to the norms."[20]

Human rights groups, however, insist that such abuse is uncalled for. "We are extremely concerned that the full extent of the humanitarian situation is being overlooked," said one group, "and that the international community is failing in its duty to . . . assure the protection of civilians in the conflict."[21]

"It's Like Hiring Someone to Do Your Dirty Work"

The aftermath of the September 11, 2001, terrorist attacks resulted in more human rights abuse, too. In the months after the attacks, U.S. soldiers took hundreds of al Qaeda operatives into custody. Many of them were imprisoned at Guantánamo Bay, a U.S. base in Cuba. However, many of the prisoners were shipped to Middle Eastern countries for interrogation.

At first, U.S. officials explained that the transfers were made simply because interrogators in those countries—Egypt, Jordan, and Syria—were more familiar with terrorist groups, their contacts, and their language than were American agents. But U.S. officials speaking privately admitted that there was a more important reason. They said that they were unable to get information from al Qaeda agents using their standard methods. The governments of Egypt, Syria, and Jordan, however, are notorious for using torture when interrogating subjects. Though it is not discussed openly, U.S. officials admitted that they need information if they are to fight the war on terror—and information flows more freely when prisoners are tortured. "We don't kick the —— out of them," one official explained. "We send them to other countries so they can kick the —— out of them."[22]

Not all intelligence officials are in favor of the practice. Some admit that the information obtained from tortured prisoners is often not true, since they might say anything just to stop the pain. Others say that it is simply wrong to

Taliban prisoners await transfer to other Middle Eastern countries for interrogation. The U.S. military sent some prisoners to countries with records of human rights violations.

knowingly send prisoners to be tortured, regardless of who is carrying it out.

The New York–based Human Rights Watch sent a letter to President George W. Bush urging him to take steps "to clarify that the use of torture is not U.S. policy."[23] Amnesty International also condemned the U.S. actions in sending prisoners to the Middle East for interrogations. One human rights worker insists that using nations with records of abusing prisoners' rights diminishes the reputation of the United States. "It's like hiring someone to do your dirty work," he says. "You're maybe not getting your own hands dirty, but you're just as guilty

as the guy you hire. The United States has to be better than that."[24]

However, the debate over how to treat prisoners exploded when it was discovered that some American troops were directly involved in the torture of prisoners in the Middle East. Although coalition forces were bound by international conventions to treat prisoners humanely, in the spring of 2004 it came to light that terrible abuses had been committed in at least one American-controlled Iraqi detention facility. Photographs surfaced showing U.S. soldiers cheerfully posing beside Iraqi prisoners who had been stripped naked and forced into uncomfortable positions or stacked in piles. Other photographs showed naked Iraqis being attacked by police dogs and otherwise terrorized or humiliated. One hooded prisoner, for example, was photographed balancing on a small box with a noose around his neck and electric wires attached to his hands; the prisoner was reportedly threatened with electrocution if he lowered his arms or fell off the box. Even more disturbing reports described the sexual abuse of inmates by soldiers, including rape.

It was unclear if a few corrupt soldiers had acted on their own initiative or if the atrocities had been sanctioned by high-ranking military officials. In any case, the abuse of prisoners was decried around the world, and many debated the morality and efficacy of such intelligence gathering practices. Even though the United States officially condemned the prisoner abuse and said it was not American policy, the long legacy of torture and abuse clearly remained alive in the Middle East.

CHAPTER 2

Women and Injustice

The human rights of women vary widely in the Middle East. While in some countries women can vote and own property, in others laws make it illegal for women to do either of those things. Some nations allow women to hold jobs outside of their homes, but in other countries that is outlawed, too.

In some Middle Eastern nations, the rights of women have changed significantly in recent years—usually with the change from one type of government to another. That is precisely what occurred in Afghanistan in the mid-1990s when the Taliban took over.

The Taliban

The Taliban, a group of religious students from conservative Muslim seminaries, or madrassas, began taking control of Afghanistan in 1994. At the time, Afghanistan was fragmented from years of war with the Soviet Union and from a subsequent civil war between corrupt Afghan warlords.

As the warlords fought over control of the country, as well as for economic gain, lawlessness prevailed. Many of the nation's highways were controlled by various warlords who charged travelers exhorbitant tolls to use them. Those who would not comply were beaten or killed. In the cities, people were assaulted and robbed in broad daylight, and women were raped on the streets. Even international relief workers, who were in Afghanistan to distribute food and medicine to people, were attacked by the warring leaders.

When the Taliban emerged in the southern provinces of Afghanistan, its members were seen as heroes by many Afghani people. The Taliban's leader,

Mohammad Omar, said later that he was inspired to challenge the warlords because of a particularly vicious crime he had heard about: Two teenage girls had been kidnapped and raped by one of the warlords and were being held prisoner in a camp. Omar and his followers attacked the camp and rescued the girls. They hanged two of the warlord's men and promised that the same would happen to other warlords who dared to attack civilians, especially women and children.

As Omar and his Taliban followers moved north, they were welcomed by many Afghans as leaders who would stand up to the warlords and others they saw as enemies of the nation. Would the Taliban rule the country wisely? Most people were unsure, but agreed that the Taliban was at least better than their current government, which could do nothing about the constant fighting among warlords. "I'd have been glad if even a dog came to power," said one villager, "if he brought peace."[25]

"I Really Don't Have a Life"

But it was soon evident that the Taliban would bring other problems to the people of Afghanistan. Its ultraconservative interpretation of the Koran

Kidnapping and Selling Women in Afghanistan

In her book The Women of Afghanistan Under the Taliban, *Rosemarie Skaine includes interviews with a number of women who experienced the Taliban's repressive regime in the late 1990s. One of these women, Fatima, tells about her experience when Taliban soldiers kidnapped her teenage daughter. Her words are reported just as they were initially translated.*

I had a very bad experience with the Taliban. . . . Scores of young girls and women have been drawn out from their houses by the Taliban and were taken to unknown destination. My 19 years daughter by the name of Simen was among those women. I shouted and begged for the Taliban to release her but the criminal gang dragged her body into the car and went away.

I then with my three children went to Kabul by foot. I asked the people over there if they have knowledge of the whereabouts of the lost women and someone told me that the Shomali women have been taken to Hilamand province . . . (where the Taliban supreme leader Mullah Omar lives). I had some money and borrowed some more from my relative and went to Hilamand. A shopkeeper told them that the Taliban bring women from Shomali and sell them to Arabs and Pakistani. I stayed two months in Hilamand, but I could not find my daughter.

I complained to the U.N. office in Kabul but they said that they are incapable of doing anything. . . . The Taliban made life a misery for us. Now I am washing clothes of other people and earn a petty amount and my three children are selling water at the bus stations.

resulted in laws that were restrictive to all citizens—but most of all, to Afghani women. And nothing symbolized those restrictions as much as the burka. No woman was permitted to step outside her home unless she was wearing the burka, a heavy, body-bag-like garment that covered every inch of her body. A two-inch-by-two-inch mesh screen in front of the eyes allowed the wearer a glimpse of her surroundings.

Although burkas had been worn by women in some of the most conservative areas of Afghanistan before the Taliban came to power, most Afghani women—especially those in the cities—had never even seen one. However, the Taliban insisted that the burka was necessary for every female Afghan over age nine because the garment protected them from men. "Women need protecting," said one official. "Burkas keep order. This tradition means women are cherished, unlike the West, where they are treated as rotten pieces of meat by men who just throw them away. If a woman wears a burka, she respects God."[26]

The vast majority of Afghani women found the burka to be uncomfortable and difficult to wear. It made them dizzy and claustrophobic. In the 90-plus-degree heat of summer, women often became overheated and nauseated because of the lack of air. More than the physical discomfort, however, women felt that the burka took away their identities. "When I put on the burqa and looked in the mirror," said one twenty-three-year-old woman, "I understood what it is the Taliban wanted: for me to realize that I am a woman and that I really don't have a life."[27]

No Education

According to one of the first Taliban decrees, girls were no longer allowed to attend school, nor could young women attend the university. By April 2000, international agencies reported that Afghanistan had the fastest-growing illiteracy rate in the world.

The ban on education was explained by the Taliban as simply a necessity, since the government claimed that the country lacked enough resources to teach all Afghani children. And because of the Taliban's strict enforcement of the separation of the sexes, Omar and his government assistants felt that boys should be the priority. Besides, as one high-ranking official noted, "Women just aren't as smart as men. They don't have the intelligence."[28]

Many Afghani girls who had already begun their studies before the Taliban's rise to power were sad. After a year or two without lessons, some said that they could barely remember what they had learned. "I used to know how to read," said one, "but I've forgotten everything."[29]

No Health Care, No Jobs

In addition to forbidding education for women, the Taliban also made it illegal for women to work outside the home. In cities such as Kabul, where women made up more than 70 percent of the teachers, more than 40 percent of the doctors, and more than half of all government workers, the ban was catastrophic. Families that had depended on two incomes struggled, and single women or widows who needed jobs were plunged into poverty.

Many women who had planned a career suddenly found themselves without a future. "This is a big disaster," said one young woman who was a second-year student at Kabul Medical Institute. "I don't know about my future. Where can I go? I damn the Taliban and the fundamentalists."[30]

Women who needed medical attention suffered too. Because the Taliban decreed that female patients could be seen only by female doctors—and because most of those had been forbidden to continue working—it was difficult for women to find treatment. Even for a toothache, a woman could

Under the Taliban, Afghani women in public were required to wear the burka, a garment that concealed every inch of their flesh.

not remove her burka to be treated by a male dentist.

"Battered Bodies, Minds, and Souls"

Human rights agencies throughout the world condemned the Taliban for its treatment of women. A spokesman for the Physicians for Human Rights observed, "We are not aware of any place in the world in recent history where women have so systematically been deprived of every opportunity to survive in the society—from working, to getting an education, to walking on the street, to getting health care."[31]

However, human rights workers stress that while Afghanistan under the Taliban was certainly the extreme, it was not the only Middle Eastern nation where women's human rights were violated. Instead, they maintain, the Taliban's human rights violations are merely one part of a continuum that includes, among others, Saudi Arabia, Jordan, Kuwait, and Palestine.

Because Afghani women were deprived of all opportunity, many resorted to begging on the streets.

Wearing a burka, a Saudi woman goes to market with her husband. Many of Saudi Arabia's strict laws violate women's rights.

In many cases, the root of the discrimination against women lies in the interpretation of the words of Islam's prophet Muhammad, who lived in the seventh century A.D. However, for his time, Muhammad had very revolutionary ideas about women's place in society. In seventh-century Arabia, for example, it was a custom to bury alive unwanted newborn girls. Those who were allowed to live were not educated or treated as more than possessions by their husbands. Muhammad condemned those practices, and taught that it was a duty for families to educate their daughters. In addition, under Islamic law women could own property and hold jobs outside the home.

Even though Muhammad's teachings as set down in the Koran were often reformist for his time, a strict interpretation of them is quite repressive by today's standards. For example, the Koran allots a daughter only half the inheritance of a son, and while a woman can testify in court, her testimony is worth only a fraction of what a man's testimony is. Today, a strict, fundamental interpretation of the Koran laws permits men to beat their wives, to restrict their movements, and to decide what they may wear in public. As religious studies professor Riffat Hassan notes, "The way Islam has been practiced in most Muslim societies for centuries has left millions of Muslim women with battered bodies, minds, and souls."[32]

Interpreting the Koran

In most Middle Eastern nations, various interpretations of the teachings of the Koran continue to dictate how women are treated. Saudi Arabia is one of the places that relies on a strict interpretation of the Koran, and is almost as repressive to women's rights as Afghanistan was under the Taliban. Women are not permitted to drive cars, nor can they walk alone, unaccompanied by a husband or male relative. Saudi women are not permitted to travel abroad unless they can produce written documentation that a brother, husband, or father authorized the trip.

An unchaperoned woman on the street can be arrested, and even women who are not Saudis are expected to follow that rule. Nieves, a young woman from the Philippines working as a maid in Riyadh, learned this the hard way. She had been invited to a birthday celebration at a restaurant. As she talked to one of the other guests—a young man—the mutawa'een, or religious police, arrested her for prostitution. Nieves was imprisoned and whipped after signing a confession written in Arabic, a language that she did not understand.

The mutawa'een have come to represent the frequent human rights violations in Saudi Arabia. They have long been criticized by human rights watch groups because of their power to punish wrongdoers—or those they suspect of wrongdoing—without benefit of a trial. "They are a law unto themselves," says one advocate. "Like their counterparts in Afghanistan, they can punish people—especially women—on the spot. They use whips, sticks, verbal abuse. I've seen reports of mutawa'een breaking off car antennas to use as weapons when they don't have anything else handy."[33]

Though they do not wear uniforms or badges, the mutawa'een are easily recognizable on the streets of Saudi cities. They wear long flowing robes and elaborate turbans unlike anything ordinary men might wear. They ride in GMC sport utility vehicles, often accompanied by a regular police officer.

Separate, but Not Equal

One of the rules enforced by the mutawa'een is the complete segregation of the sexes in Saudi Arabia. Girls attend separate schools when they are young and, if they continue their studies, can attend a women's university. Women go to segregated library rooms and do their banking at women-only branches. Women can work outside the home, but they are steered toward jobs that allow them to be separated from men, such as teaching and nursing.

The separation of the sexes does not necessarily mean that women are discriminated against if the facilities for men and women are equal. However, that is not the case in many parts of Saudi Arabia. Schools for girls are typically of a poorer quality than those for boys. And libraries for women rarely have computers or reference materials that men have in their libraries.

Even in restaurants owned by Western companies, the separate-but-not-equal rule applies. McDonald's, Pizza Hut, and Starbucks all have separate zones for male and female customers, and staff enforce the rules. As one visitor to a Saudi city noted, there is a noticeable difference in the eating areas:

In Saudi Arabia, even Western-owned restaurants like this McDonald's in a Riyadh shopping mall must provide separate sections for men and women.

Saudi Arabia's strict dress code requires women in public to cover their clothing with a black cloak known as an abaya.

The men's sections are typically lavish, comfortable, and up to Western standards, whereas the women's or families' sections are often run-down, neglected and, in the case of Starbucks, have no seats. Worse, these firms will bar entrance [even] to Western women who show up without their husbands.[34]

Veil and *Abaya*

As in many other Middle Eastern countries, women in Saudi Arabia are required by law to obey a dress code. Although they are permitted to wear whatever they like at home, they must cover their clothing with a long black cloak called an *abaya* while in public. In addition, they have to wear a head scarf and veil, which covers their hair and most of their face.

Many women do not mind wearing the *abaya* and veil, but say they resent the *mutawa'een* enforcing it. "It's part of my religion that I cover myself," says one twenty-six-year-old woman, who moved to the United States six years ago to attend school. "It's a modesty issue, and I'm fine with that. But in Riyadh, where I grew up, the *mutawa'een* take the enforcement of the rule too far. No one should be beaten or arrested for how she is dressed. That's what I think."[35]

Teenage girls in Saudi Arabia maintain that the religious police treat them unfairly, patrolling areas outside beauty shops or women's clothing stores in hopes of finding young women breaking the rules. They especially look for those whose veils do not completely cover their heads, and when they find such a woman, they verbally assault her. "They attack women with harsh words," says a Saudi teenager, "like, 'You sinner, don't you fear punishment in the heareafter? Cover your head properly or we'll take you in the GMC.'"[36]

Intermediate School No. 31

The gender discrimination of the Saudi religious police was the subject of international outrage in 2002 when their extreme enforcement of the dress code resulted in the deaths of fifteen girls. On March 11, 2002, a fire broke out in Intermediate School No. 31, a girls' school in Mecca. It was a building designed for 250, but more than 800 girls were attending school there.

Like other girls' schools, it was inferior to most boys' schools; it lacked up-to-date supplies and educational materials as well as basic safety features. There was no fire alarm in the building, no fire extinguishers, and no emergency exits. Also, as with other girls' schools in Saudi Arabia, it was kept locked (from the inside as well as the outside) when school was in session. As one Arab journalist explains, the procedure for opening the door is not a simple one:

> Female students and teachers are locked in a building surrounded by high walls which protect them from men's eyes. . . . The buildings normally have only one exit, and the key is in the care of a gate-keeper. . . . In case of a fire in one of these schools, the headmistress must first call the [Department of

Girls' Education] to get permission to summon the fire department.[37]

After the fire broke out and the headmistress finally got permission to call the fire department, a group of *mutawa'een* arrived on the scene. When the religious police saw that the frightened girls trying to escape were not wearing their veils and *abayas*, they instructed the firefighters to not allow the girls to come out of the building.

"It Is Sinful to Approach Them"

One fireman tried to explain to the *mutawa'een* that it was an emergency. "We told them the situation was dangerous and it was not the time to discuss religious issues," he said, "but they refused and started shouting at us. . . . Whenever the girls got out through the main gate, these people forced them to return via another. Instead of extending a helping hand for the rescue work, they were using their hands to beat us."[38]

Not only were the religious police not allowing the girls to get out of the burning building, but they prevented anyone else from helping the girls. Fathers who were trying to get past the police to save their daughters were stopped by *mutawa'een* who told the men, "It is sinful to approach them."[39]

Fifteen girls between the ages of thirteen and seventeen were trampled to death that morning, and fifty-two other students and teachers were injured. As details of the tragedy spread, people around the world were horrified and condemned the Saudi religious police's actions. Said one representative of Human Rights Watch, "State authorities with direct and indirect responsibility for this tragedy must be held accountable."[40]

Public sentiment was strongly anti-*mutawa'een*. The Saudi press condemned the police's actions—criticism that was almost unheard of. Voicing the anger and frustration that many Saudi citizens felt, one Saudi newspaper editorial urged the government to take a closer look at the gender discrimination in the country that allows such things to occur. Insisting that the trouble was not Islam but, rather, politics, he wrote, "Saudi males must open their minds and broaden their horizons."[41]

Violence Against Women

Not all human rights violations against women occur at the hands of religious police or government, however. In fact, a startling amount of violence against women happens in the home. The Koran, in the fourth sura, or chapter, decrees what husbands are allowed to do when their wives are rebellious or insubordinate: "You shall first talk to them, then you may use negative incentives like deserting them in bed, then you may beat them."[42] So widespread is wife beating throughout the Middle East that social workers have encountered many women who feel that such abuse is acceptable because Islam allows it.

Certainly one of the most extreme examples of violence against women in the Middle East is a practice known

The Women of Saudi Arabia

In an editorial written for the November 24, 2003, edition of the Financial Times, *Isobel Coleman argues that the Saudi government is long overdue in granting rights to the women who live there. The following is an excerpt from that editorial.*

Saudi Arabia urgently needs reform. . . . Reformists would do well to start with the municipal elections promised for next year. They should push for women to be allowed to vote and to run for office. Enfranchisement of women would not only represent a welcome advance in human rights, but could also begin a process of real social reform. . . .

Saudi women are poised for change. Only a generation ago, less than 2 percent of them were literate. Today, more than 70 percent are, thanks to free public education for girls which started in 1964, against strong conservative resistance. By some accounts, female students now outnumber male students at schools and universities, which remain segregated. Saudi women today are not allowed to drive, are subject to beatings from the vice squad for "morality lapses", such as appearing in public without full cover of the abaya, and are routinely treated as second-class citizens. . . .

Saudi women increasingly chafe under the restrictions imposed on them. Prominent professional women have petitioned the government for elections, an independent judiciary, protection of human rights and religious tolerance. As the language of human rights becomes more common, awareness is growing about the importance of woman's rights.

Although women in Saudi Arabia have enjoyed the right to an education since 1964, campuses throughout the country remain segregated.

Human rights advocates read the Koran at the grave of a victim of an honor killing, an ancient tribal practice allowing male relatives to kill women who dishonor their families.

as "honor killing." It is based on the ancient tribal culture in which a family's honor was determined by the purity of its women. Therefore, a woman who has a sexual relationship before marriage, or one who is raped, or even a woman who marries a man not approved by her father is a blot on the family's honor. When that happens, the woman may be killed by a male relative to regain the honor of the family.

"A Few Weeks Later I See Them Again, Dead"

Although it is an ancient idea, honor killings are still carried out in the Middle East. Many nations have laws that forbid honor killings, but few men who commit such murders are prosecuted. Experts say that there may be anywhere between five hundred and one thousand honor killings in the Middle East each year. It is difficult to know for certain because the deaths are often officially listed as suicides or un-solved murders.

One Jordanian doctor says that he sees honor killings with alarming frequency. "Women are brought to me [by their families] to be examined after a sexual assault," he says. "I tell their parents they are innocent, but a few weeks later I see them again, dead."[43]

Not every victim of an honor crime is killed, however. One ten-year-old girl let a neighbor into the house when no one else was home. Pretending he wanted to borrow sugar, the man attacked and raped the child. "When he was on his way out, my mother and eldest brother came home," the girl told relief workers. "They both started beating me. They were both yelling, *Inshallah tmuti'*—It's best for you to die."[44]

The girl was not killed by her family, though she was forced to marry the neighbor as a way of preserving the family's honor. Notes author Sally Armstrong, she became "a prisoner in her own home until she was fourteen and old enough to be married off to the offending [neighbor]. She never saw her playmates or attended school again, and to this day blames herself for opening the door."[45]

Some victims are simply abandoned by their family, who hope that no one learns of their daughter's lost virginity. One nine-year-old Iraqi girl who had been raped was brought to the doctor by her father. He wanted a medical report on whether she was technically a virgin. Since she was not, the girl was left in an orphanage.

Fighting Back

Though some officials say that the number of honor killings has increased in recent years, there has also been an increase in the number of people who want to see the practice stopped. Nadera Shalhoub-Kevorkian, a Palestinian criminologist and social worker, says that the idea of honor killings should not have any place in Islam. But to change things, she says, is not easy:

I love my culture and I know how to change what's wrong with it. . . . Our society is in transition. The codes of conduct aren't clear. Some people are trying to move backward to preserve the norm; others are moving forward. In the process, there's more attention to crimes against women, more willingness to help [as well as] more cases of women being killed and more fear.[46]

One young woman from Iran believes that women must help themselves, too. If women are to stop being victims in Islamic society, she says, they must stop being afraid to show their strength: "I feel that the more we learn, the better citizens we can be. The world shouldn't be men against women. It also should not be men feeling as though they must protect women, like we are glass statues that could break. Women don't need to be like that."[47]

Improvement in Iran

In fact, Iran is an example of a Middle Eastern nation where women have fought for—and often won—rights for

"What Would He Do?"

Honor killing has been on the increase in some places in the Middle East. In her book Veiled Threat: The Hidden Power of the Women of Afghanistan, *Sally Armstrong describes her meeting with a Palestinian doctor in East Jerusalem where she discovers that the deadly practice has deep roots.*

Getting away with [honor killing] is disturbingly easy. Dr. Jalal Alijabri, director of the Forensic Medical Center for the Palestinian Authority in East Jerusalem, says he hardly ever sees a case in which honor killing is the official cause of death. "In our culture, everybody knows but nobody says. I get cases that say the cause of death is a firearm injury. I know inside what really happened but what can I do? I sign the certificate and say, Bye-bye; that's it."

Dr. Alijabri exemplifies the "enlightened" Palestinian man. Ask him about the price women sometimes pay for safeguarding the family's name and he's strongly against honor killing. Ask him about his own family and the tone changes. He's the father of eight, five boys and three girls. What would he do if one of his daughters became pregnant and wasn't married? He's aghast at the question. "A girl knows she cannot be pregnant. She cannot have sexual relations. She must understand what would happen."

So what would he do? "I don't know," he replies.

themselves. After the shah was ousted and replaced with an Islamic government, women had fewer rights. Though the Ayatollah Khomeini's interpretation of the Koran was not as fundamentalist as the Taliban's would be, there were limits that had not been in place before. Segregation of the sexes meant that girls could no longer go to school with boys. Women were discouraged from working outside the home. Those who wanted to work found that they could not serve as judges, for example, or as department heads or administrators at universities in Iran.

However, many women challenged such limits. A number of women's reformist groups worked hard to make their dissatisfaction known. Women could vote, and although the conservative clerics controlled much of the government, they slowly gained some of the things they had lost during the revolution of 1979. A few concessions have been made, including a higher quality of job choices and better schools.

Woman's rights became very publicized in 2003 when an Iranian woman named Shirin Ebadi was awarded the Nobel Peace Prize for her struggle for human rights in Iran and around the world. Ebadi has focused especially on gaining rights for women and children, saying that no society deserves to be counted as civilized unless their women and children are treated with respect.

The fact that Ebadi has worked as an Iranian lawyer, judge, lecturer, writer, and activist is a testament to how much women have gained in modern-day Iran.

Despite these gains, Behnaz Arsanali, a woman from Tehran who started her own furniture company, continues to be hassled by religious police in Iran. She is not surprised, she says, because the nation continues to be run by conservative men. "Patriarchy is a basic part of our culture," Arsanali explains. "And the law, unfortunately, backs men up." However, she is proud of what she and other women have done in expanding their roles in Iran. "We are all paving our own road now," she says. "No one gave us anything in this regime. Whatever progress Iranian women have made has been because of our own persistence and hard work."[48]

CHAPTER 3

The Right of Expression

Another of the human rights declared by the United Nations is that of self-expression. No one should be denied the right to have an opinion, or the right to express that opinion without being censored or coerced by the government. Yet that is precisely what is happening throughout the Middle East, where people risk their lives daily by being critical of their governments' leaders or policies.

"You Could End Up in Prison, or Even Dead"

Many of these critics are journalists. Most Middle Eastern nations have government-controlled news, a system in which political officials control what gets printed or aired on television. And while some journalists are willing to follow government regulations, many are not.

"To be a journalist is not to work for somebody, not completely," says one Iranian journalism student.

You may work for a newspaper or magazine, but as a writer, your thoughts are your own. It is a job that allows you to look at a situation from your own perspective, and offer your own thoughts on what you see. And well, if the powers that be don't like you, you'd better hope that you're a journalist who lives in the United States or another free country. [The Middle East] is the worst place to be critical of government. You could end up in prison, or even dead.[49]

Experts agree, saying that the heavy-handed treatment of journalists in the Middle East has been steadily worsening.

A Journalist Jailed

Journalists expressing opinions that are critical of the government are jailed in Iran. The following excerpt from "Journalist Given One Year Suspended Sentence" in BBC Monitoring Media demonstrates how seriously Iran's rulers view the actions of a writer named Emadoldin Baghi.

Reporters Without Borders today voiced outrage at the suspended sentence of one year in prison which the sixth revolutionary court of Tehran has passed on journalist Emadoldin Baghi without making public its reason. . . . Baghi, who worked for *Newhat*, a daily closed down by the authorities, was tried on November 9 [2003]. . . .

This threat is clearly an attempt to silence Baghi, who often writes about violations of freedom of expression in Iran for the reformist dailies *Shargh* and *Yas-e-no*.

"I was unable to defend myself in this travesty of a trial which lasted only a few minutes, and I was barely able to speak," Baghi told Reporters Without Borders. "What kind of trial is it where there is neither lawyer nor judge, or where the judge is prosecutor at the same time and where the defendant is not even told of the charges against him?"

In his book *The Tragedy of Democracy in Iran*, Baghi accused the Iranian authorities of being involved in a series of murders of intellectuals and journalists in 1998. He has already been imprisoned because of his articles in the reformist press. In his most recent previous trial . . . he was given a three-year prison sentence for "threatening national security."

Journalist Emadoldin Baghi has been jailed numerous times for speaking out against human rights violations in Iran.

A Saudi man reads a newspaper story about Saddam's capture. The governments of many Middle Eastern countries control the media.

"The only change [in recent years]," says one Saudi news editor, "is that governments have become better at breaking our pens."[50] Indeed, the number of imprisoned journalists throughout the region has grown significantly in the past five years—with Iran the most notorious.

Iran is sometimes called "the largest jail for journalists"[51] because of its repressive policies toward free speech and expression. In 2003 there were twenty journalists in prison there, many detained without trial or access to lawyers. Their sentences range from four months to twelve years.

Writer Emadoldin Baghi was released in October 2003 after spending more than two years in prison. Baghi had been jailed after writing an editorial criticizing Iran's death penalty. Soon after his release, government authorities notified Baghi that he would face new charges because of a book he had written about the government's role in the murder of political protesters since the 1979 revolution.

"They don't just jail journalists," says one young Iranian man. "They kill newspapers. Dozens and dozens of them have been shut down by the government because they call for reforms or they write about something that the conservatives don't like."[52] One daily newspaper was closed down in May 2002, for example, because it had reviewed a book about women musicians in Iran. According to government officials, the article was "offensive to the sacred principles of Islam."[53]

A Government Mouthpiece

Many journalists maintain that the press in Arab nations has been forced to serve a different function than that in many Western countries. Instead of seeking out answers to questions or investigating stories in order to learn the truth, journalists in Middle Eastern nations are there to serve the government. Many newspapers are licensed or owned by the government. In Saudi Arabia, for example, of the dozen newspapers published, most are owned by the royal family.

In the Palestinian territories of the West Bank and Gaza Strip, too, the media remains under the control of government officials, and reporters are automatically expected to be a mouthpiece for Palestinian leaders. This makes true journalism very difficult. As one reporter explains, "Palestinian journalists have to be very careful. You're not supposed to anger the government, or touch on sensitive issues, and if you do, you are taking a risk."[54]

In Saudi Arabia, all the newspapers are forced to follow two important rules: First, nothing critical can be said about Islam, and second, there can be nothing that reflects badly on any member of the royal family. Any story that might seem to touch on those subjects must first be cleared with the Saudi Ministry of Information.

A Break in Protocol

There have been breaks in the protocol, however. After the 2002 fire in which fifteen Saudi girls were killed, Saudi newspapers dared to be critical of the government. Says one observer,

> The Saudi press made history by writing about the fire without first asking the Ministry of Information for permission. For several weeks, the government stood aside and simply let the press be free. . . . By Saudi standards, the coverage was so relentless that even reformists were troubled. Eventually, the Interior Minister summoned the editors-in-chief of all the newspapers in the country and told them that the stories must stop. They immediately did.[55]

One American journalist visited Saudi Arabia after that occasion. After observing a newsroom in action and seeing the strict rules the press is required to follow, he asked a reporter what role the press might have in helping Saudi Arabia become a better country. "I don't think the press can play a role," the man said honestly. "I don't see a single paper calling for reform. The papers are not structured in a way to make that possible."[56]

An Opportunity to Change?

There have been a few times in recent history where political writers in the Middle East were optimistic that things could change. A popular Saudi Arabian journalist named Hussein Shobokshi was one of those writers who hoped that his government might allow the press what he believed was some much-needed freedom. In a July 2003 column for a large Saudi newspaper called *Okaz*, Shobokshi took a chance.

He wrote a bedtime story, as told to his young daughter, describing a future where she could drive a car and work as a lawyer, and where all people could vote. Most readers were delighted by the piece, but the powerful conservatives in government were furious. As a result, the editors at *Okaz* were ordered to drop Shobokshi's column.

Even in Middle Eastern nations that are known for being more modern and more Westernized, freedom of expression for journalists is rarely evident. In Kuwait, for example, whose capital, Kuwait City, has been described as looking more like Houston, Texas, than a Middle Eastern city, there are laws forbidding freedom of expression. One Kuwaiti journalist was arrested in 2003 because he criticized the government leader, Sheikh Jabir Ahmed Sabah—a crime punishable by five years in prison.

Artistic Expression

Just as Middle Eastern governments often deny political expression, they limit artistic expression, too. Dancers, musicians, poets, and other artists are monitored for any works that may be offensive to governmental or religious leaders.

For example, one of Saddam Hussein's first acts as president of Iraq was to put the nation's artists under the control of his political party, the Baathists. That way, he could make sure that what was created could be strictly censored so that any material about him was always presented in a positive light. Poets and songwriters were urged to create works praising Saddam's life, and for those who complied, there was a fortune to be made. Those who refused, however, found themselves in danger. "Failure to do Saddam's bidding," explains Saddam biographer Con Coughlin, "often resulted in imprisonment and torture, frequently ending in death for hundreds of Iraqi writers and intellectuals."[57]

Within a few years, there were more than two hundred songs that had been written about him. Each night Iraqi television stations would play what was

Journalist Hussein Shobokshi displays some of the hate mail he received after he published a story in a Saudi newspaper that advocated women's rights.

known as "the Saddam song," which was one of his favorites:

> Oh Saddam, our victorious,
> Oh Saddam, our beloved,
> You carry the nation's dawn
> between your eyes;
> Oh Saddam, everything is good
> with you,
> Allah, Allah, we are happy; Saddam lights our days . . . [58]

"Don't . . . Ban My Movies"

Saddam's heavy-handed control of the arts in Iraq was to strengthen his control of the nation. Other Middle Eastern countries, however, censor art that they deem un-Islamic. For instance, in Egypt, which is home to the largest film industry in the Middle East, movies are coming more and more under the scrutiny of the religious conservatives.

Iraqi girls sing pro–Saddam Hussein songs at a rally. The Iraqi government encouraged musicians to compose songs praising Saddam.

Historically, Egypt has been generally liberal in its handling of the arts. However, in recent years it has been the citizens, rather than the government, who are increasingly conservative about their religion. To appease people, government censors evaluate all movies made or shown in the country. Many, especially those made in the United States, are banned. *The Matrix Reloaded*, for example, could not be shown because censors felt that it questioned the nature of God. Many others are banned because of violence or sex between unmarried people.

Many Egyptian screenwriters and directors are angry about the level of censorship, for they say that it makes creativity impossible. "Disagree with me," says one director, "but don't confiscate my opinions or ban my movies."[59] However, censors explain that they are just following the trend of society in general. They point to a showing of the American film *American Beauty* a few years ago in Cairo. During a brief nude scene in the movie, many in the audience shouted and stood up in protest. "In the back of every censor's mind is society," explains Ali Abu Shadi, head of Egypt's Censorship Board. "The state itself seems to be unable to deal with society right now. The level of conservatism is very high."[60]

Censoring Theater in Iran

Iran experienced that same conservatism after the revolution of 1979, when ultraconservative Muslim clerics took over Iran's government. Immediately after the revolution there was a nationwide movement to suppress art that clerics felt was dangerous to the morals of the people. That suppression continues today.

Rehearsals of theater productions, for instance, are attended by clerics who take notes on scenes and dialogue they feel is inappropriate. Directors are often ordered to make changes to such things before opening night. One frustrated director complained that he had been forced to rewrite scenes over and over, and the clerics were still not happy with the result. "I don't know

Saddam and Art

The article "Iraqi President Meets Artists, Discusses Censorship," in BBC Monitoring Middle East, *describes a 2002 meeting between Saddam Hussein and a group of the most prominent Iraqi theater and movie actors, directors, and writers. The following excerpt demonstrates Saddam's insistence on controlling what topics are acceptable for plays and movies within the country.*

Amid applause, Saddam said: "I am meeting with you just to tell you that we are ready to extend all kinds of support to you. . . . True, we need the serious theatre, but there is nothing wrong in smiling without indecency, without undermining our people's higher values and without harming the social fabric, which we need as an asset for us in order to maintain the great momentum and realize the major targets that we see on the horizon. . . .

"We smile as we see our great ability to remain steadfast. We smile when we see the great spirit of martyrdom among our people in defense of their great aims. By smile, I mean a salute for them. We salute life because we are still living; we make life. . . . We should view the non-serious theatre as an interlude for rest and not for amusement. By this I mean an interlude to provide relief for us in order to proceed forward and not to divert attention to the uphill tasks."

when they'll give us their decision," he said. "They come to rehearsals, they watch, then they go away. Then they come again, they watch, and go away. We may be rehearsing forever."[61]

Often it is not only the religious leaders who insist on theatrical performances meeting the standards of conservative Islam. One production of Tennessee Williams's *The Glass Menagerie* was challenged in 1995 when male students angrily wrote to the conservative newspaper *Islamic Republic*, protesting that the man and woman onstage had not only lit cigarettes but touched. "The female and male entered into very vulgar contact," they wrote. "We still haven't recovered from the shock when an actor and an actress embraced very tightly."[62]

Music, Dancing, and Movies in Iran

There have been strict rules for other forms of art in post-1979 Iran as well. Iran's most popular singer, Googoosh, who sang melancholy songs about love and separation, was given a choice when the Ayatollah Khomeini came to power. Because of the sensual nature of her voice, she was told she must leave Iran forever or stop singing. She chose the latter (although she has recently decided to do concerts in other parts of the world).

It is a testament to her enormous talent that even though she has been banned from doing concerts or recording new records, people for years have risked fines and even imprisonment to buy bootlegged copies of her records at kiosks in cities throughout Iran. "A wedding without Googoosh's voice," notes one observer, "is unthinkable."[63]

Dance is outlawed in Iran also because of its provocative nature. In one much-publicized case, a forty-six-year-old Iranian American named Mohammad Khordadian was arrested in Iran in July 2002 for the crime of dancing. Khordadian lived in Los Angeles and made his living as a dancer, performing a combination of salsa and belly dancing. After learning that his mother had died, he returned to Iran and was promptly arrested and charged with promoting corruption among young people. That crime carries a ten-year jail sentence and a lifetime ban on teaching or performing dance, no matter where he lives.

Movies, too, have undergone an enormous amount of censorship. American and European films—favorites of the Iranian people—have been banned. And it has been difficult for Iranian filmmakers to make films that conform to the conservative standards of the clerics.

The king of Iranian comedy, a chubby-cheeked man with a walrus mustache, is Akbar Abdi. The Iranian Ministry of Culture banned Abdi's movie *The Snowman* in 1995. The religious censors objected to the plot, which follows a man from Iran trying to get a visa to the United States. What got the film banned was that the main character, played by Abdi, disguised himself by dressing as a woman.

"I was the Tootsie or Mrs. Doubtfire of Iran," said Abdi later. "It was a won-

The Age of Googoosh

The Iranian pop singer Googoosh was banned from performing after the 1979 revolution when the Ayatollah Khomeini's regime deemed her music unsuitable for conservative Muslims. In 2000 a slightly less conservative government allowed her to perform in other countries, and as a result, people are learning about a part of Iran's history. The following excerpt is from an article titled, "The Age of Googoosh."

Banned from singing in public for two decades, the news that Googoosh, now 50, would be heard again on a North American concert tour spread like fire on the international grapevine. For Iranians abroad, her comeback . . . is a reminder of feelings long-suppressed and of a cultural void that was never properly filled. . . . "After all these years, why are we still hung up on Googoosh?" wondered the owner of an Iranian grocery in San Jose, California, who has done brisk trade in Googoosh tickets. . . .

For today's young Iranians, who know her music only through recordings, Googoosh is a symbol of what it was like to live before the revolution: in a Tehran of miniskirts and discos, a country as lawless as today, but more open to the world and to fun. . . .

This is her power; the woman who encompasses for Iranians the resistance of John Lennon, the sensuous tragedy of Marilyn Monroe and the fame of Elvis. That hers has remained the voice of Iran throughout two violent political eras is testament that Iranians feel closer to one another than either they, or their governments, have ever realized.

Banned from performing in Iran since 1979, pop star Googoosh has recently begun touring in other countries.

derful part. A man trying to be a woman is one of three roles every actor wants to play. The other two are an addict and a crazy person."[64] The movie was banned until 1997, when a slightly more liberal leader was elected president of Iran.

Even though the film was allowed, however, many conservative Muslims in the country still did not want the film shown. Bands of extremists attacked local theaters, breaking windows in nearby shops and ripping down advertisements for the film. People standing in line for tickets were physically attacked as well.

The Snowman was eventually shown in many theaters in Iran, and became a favorite among Iranian audiences. However, even with a more liberal president, the conservative clerics who control Iran's legislature have enacted strict laws for moviemakers. As with theatri-cal performances, censors have to approve all projects from the beginning to the final cuts. They believe it is wrong for a woman to appear in a movie without the full head and body covering— even if she is portrayed in her home. Islamic censors also believe that violence has no place in a movie.

The Most Conservative of All
While Iran's rules dictating the acceptable forms of artistic expression may

Taliban soldiers burn banned movies in a bonfire. The Taliban banned all artistic expression that was not religious.

seem repressive, they do not even compare to those in Afghanistan under the Taliban. When the Taliban came to power, it did not bother with the process of censorship; it simply banned all artistic expression that was not religious.

Music, explained Taliban officials, was prohibited because it was simply against the rules of Islam. They claimed that there was a little-known directive from the prophet Muhammad telling people that they dare not listen to music "lest molten lead be poured into their ears on judgement day."[65] As a demonstration of how serious they were about banning music, Taliban religious police set up checkpoints and searched cars for cassette tapes. Outside Kabul, there were signposts draped with shiny brown tape that had been confiscated from cars and taxis.

The only music allowed in Afghanistan was tapes of tuneless religious chants by the Taliban. Songs with titles such as "The Taliban Arrived and Ruled" and "Taliban, O Taliban, You're Creating Facilities; You're Defeating Enemies" were little consolation for Afghans who were used to rock and folk music from Pakistan and India. One disgusted music lover said that he resented the way the government dictated what people listened to. "I hate this society," he said. "Everyone does."[66]

"This Is a Country Without a Culture"

Many Afghans agreed, saying that music had always been an integral part of daily life. Musicians, especially, were up-set. The streets of Kabul, Afghanistan's capital, were crowded with out-of-work musicians begging for money for firewood. One of Afghanistan's most famous singers, Seddiq Qiam, said that he hid his instruments at a friend's house so that the Taliban police could not destroy them. "I'm afraid," he said. "I'm without my music. I can't live like this."[67]

The bans extended to visual arts, too. Islam forbids drawings or paintings showing the human face because it is considered idolatry. As a result, the Taliban destroyed all art in which people's faces (or even the faces of animals) were seen. Sometimes the religious police merely cut out the faces or painted over them and left the rest of the painting. One visitor to a hotel in Kabul soon after the Taliban's rise to power was struck by the oddness of the result:

> On the landing of the stairs two floors down, there was a large landscape painting, about sixteen feet by twelve feet, of a pond, some flowers, a forest and a few animals. The heads of the three animals had been cut out of the painting to comply with Taliban aesthetic restrictions. . . . This left a decapitated deer standing by a pond and a headless beaver sitting on a tree stump.[68]

The nation's new antiart posture was as alarming to some Afghans as its ban of music. The president of Afghanistan's Central Union of Artists was concerned that a lack of art would be a severe loss for an already troubled society. "This is

An Afghani woman displays paintings destroyed by the Taliban. The Taliban ordered the destruction of all artwork depicting human or animal faces.

a country without a culture," he said. "Any country without culture is not a country."[69] Even after the Taliban was ousted from power in 2001, in fact, many of the restrictions it introduced remained in place in some parts of the country.

Waging War on Artistic Expression

Just as in Afghanistan under the Taliban, fundamentalist Islam has dealt with artistic expression in Saudi Arabia in a very oppressive manner. It was not always like this; in fact, the roots of artistic suppression go back to only 1979.

It was then that a large group of Muslim extremists—most of them students—staged a massive protest against the royal family's ties with Europe and the United States. The protesters took control of Mecca's Grand Mosque, which resulted in two weeks of bloody fighting with Saudi soldiers. More than 120 soldiers died, and 63 of the rebels were beheaded—the largest mass execution ever held in Saudi Arabia.

Even though the mosque was reclaimed and the protesters executed afterward, the royal family realized that it was crucial to give in to the increasingly angry fundamentalists within the country. As one of the first concessions, notes one observer, the ultraconservative Islamic clerics, "with their fear of outside influences, waged war on art and the pleasures of the intellect."[70]

Music was one of the first victims of the new conservative laws, and it became illegal. Although the capital city of Riyadh built a multimillion-dollar concert hall, no musical performances have been given there. No street musicians are allowed to play, and no Saudi television station is allowed to air any form of musical entertainment. Businesses are prohibited from having music play when callers are on hold.

"Almost as if it Were Pornography"

The visual arts have taken a beating in Saudi Arabia, too. Although painting is not banned, the Saudi clerics have enacted the same laws the Taliban did that prohibit any representation of the faces of human beings or animals. Artists are limited to abstract paintings, still lifes, or landscapes. Interestingly, the ban includes commercial art as well. Starbucks, which has branches throughout Saudi Arabia, was told that it could no longer feature its logo, a long-haired woman wearing a crown, on its signs. To com-

ply, Starbucks changed its logo there to a simple crown.

The effect of the law on painting and sculpture, however, was immense. Museums that had previously housed some of the greatest works in the Middle East were emptied of all but landscapes and geometric abstracts. One visitor to Saudi Arabia went to Riyadh's famous National Museum and found one extremely old painting showing a human face, although the artwork was in a most unusual place:

> In one of the grand halls, I noticed an odd cul-de-sac, under a stairwell, where I found a painting of a human face—the only one in the museum. It was a wall drawing from the village of Al Fao, from the second or third century A.D., depicting a man with a garland around his curly hair. . . . I suppose it was a tribute to the importance of this miniature portrait that it was displayed at all; still, to be hidden under the stairs, almost as if it were pornography, made me admire as never before the power of the human form.[71]

Internet Controls

With such restrictive rules on what they are allowed to see and read, many Middle Eastern people have been very interested in exploring the world of the Internet. Although a few Middle Eastern nations such as Jordan, Israel, and the United Arab Emirates have uncensored access to the Internet, people in several nations have found that the same government controls that banned certain films and books kept them from accessing the Web.

During the regime of Saddam Hussein, for instance, Iraq did not have Internet access available to its citizens. The official government position then was that the Internet was "one of the American means to enter every house in the world."[72] Although the government did not ban Internet use per se, it made possession of a modem—a must for hooking one's computer to the Web—illegal. Even without such laws, however, the physical damage to Iraq's power stations and electrical transmitters during the Gulf War made computer use difficult. After the fall of Saddam's regime in 2003, the interim government promised to make repairs so that citizens could use the Internet.

The Saudi Arabian government does allow its citizens to use the Internet. But it has installed technological systems that limit the sites Saudis may access. Government officials explain that such limits are necessary for the good of the Islamic society. "We have programs, software, and hardware," said one official, "that prevent the entry of material that corrupts or that harms our Muslim values, tradition, and culture."[73]

Syria has similar concerns for its citizens, and has been reluctant to allow Internet access to its people. The gov-

The window of a Starbucks location in Riyadh, Saudi Arabia, shows the company's logo without the familiar, long-haired, bare-breasted siren.

Students at a Baghdad university learn to access the Internet in 2004. Many Middle Eastern countries restrict access to the Internet.

ernment worries what communication from the West may do to the Syrian people—especially its young people. "Our problem is . . . we are a traditional society," says one computer spokesman, "and we have to know if there is something that cannot fit with our society. We have to make it safe."[74]

Satellite Television: A Window to the World

It is television that has allowed many citizens of repressive governments to view the outside world. Though most Middle Eastern governments control local television stations, satellite dishes have opened up a great many options for people in Saudi Arabia, Iraq, and Iran. Satellite dishes are technically illegal, of course. Religious leaders have issued fatwas, or holy denouncements, condemning the technology. Religious police carry guns and, when they see a satellite dish perched on the roof of a home, are permitted by law to shoot it. However, there are simply too many people who demand them, and who are willing to take the risk of a fine and having their equipment seized. Owners have become skilled at making their dishes less visible by installing them in a courtyard or disguising them as grills or air conditioners.

Many say that the programming they get is worth the risk. They are tired of the constant religious programs seen on local channels, which consist of hours and hours of prayers. With satellites, people in the Middle East are exposed to a wide range of television programs—from Disney Channel movies to Smackdown wrestling and gangsta rap videos, from reruns of '70s sitcoms to women's programming.

One Saudi understands that there are many programs that may offend some people, especially the most traditional members of society. However, he believes that most people are excited by the entertainment choices available with satellite. "It's broadened the view of the people," he says. "You can watch the world."[75]

CHAPTER 4

Children's Rights

C hildren are the most vulnerable members of any society, yet the violation of their human rights is often less visible than that of adults. As one human rights worker notes, "Children tend to be quieter about the abuse or ill-treatment they receive, and they are usually willing to accept unfair—even painful—situations because they don't know any better."[76]

While other human rights violations in the Middle East occur either because of very conservative interpretations of Islam or because of politically repressive leaders, the violation of children's rights usually occurs for a different reason. In millions of cases throughout the Middle East, children's rights are violated for economic reasons.

"When you have a region where poverty is an epidemic, where even little kids have to work to put food on their family's table, you have instant hu-

man rights violations," says one New York human rights worker. "The UN has agreed that education is a right for all children, but that isn't happening for millions of kids. How can you go to school when you're picking crops ten hours a day or working in a brick factory?"[77]

Reality Versus the Law

Egypt's Nile Delta is one region where children are working instead of attending school. The Delta contains the most fertile soil on earth, and prized Egyptian cotton is grown in fields throughout the area. It is children who pick the cotton there during the fall harvest. When cotton is not in season, they pick potatoes or jasmine.

There are laws in Egypt prohibiting child labor. Supposedly all Egyptian children must attend school until they are fifteen years old. The law further

Young girls pick cotton in Egypt's Nile Delta. Despite laws prohibiting child labor, many children in the delta are forced to work.

stipulates that no child can work more than part-time so that the work will not interfere with the child's studies. However, as millions of Egyptian children know firsthand, there is a big difference between what the law says and what really happens. In fact, it is the Egyptian government's Agriculture Ministry, which owns about 10 percent of the nation's cotton crop, that hires the children.

In the town of Sul Hagar, located in the Nile Delta, families are very poor.

Unemployment among the men in town runs between 30 and 40 percent. Those who have jobs are field workers, and if they are lucky, their children will find work in the fields too. Though there is a small school that the children could attend, the majority of parents need the extra income their children can supply.

For eight hours of hot, back-numbing work, a cotton picker makes $1.50 per day. The children—all between ten and fifteen years old—rise at dawn to catch a ride on a large truck that will take them to the cotton fields. One observer noted how cramped and crowded the trucks become, as more than 150 children try to find a spot to sit for the journey. "Early risers win it all," some of them sing. "Early risers win it all."[78]

Once at their assigned field, the children spread out into work squads, each with its own overseer. The overseer's job is to make sure the children stay focused on their work, and that often means quelling any talking or singing the workers do. Reporter Emad Mekay observed a supervisor waving a stick at a bunch of children who were singing as they picked the cotton. Threatening to hit them, he yelled, "You shut up, you daughters of dogs. You shut up, I said."[78]

Fifteen-year-old Hanan Ali says that she does not feel cheated because she works full-time and cannot get an education. The oldest of six children, Hanan and her father—a street sweeper—are the breadwinners in her family. "I have to work harder," Hanan says. "I get more money if I pick more cotton. I never went to school, and I do not expect I ever will now. It is necessary to work, and we accept whatever God gives us."[80]

A supervisor uses a cane to urge children picking cotton in one of the Nile Delta's fields to work faster.

"What Has Happened Has Burned Our Hearts"

In addition to depriving children of an education, full-time work in the fields can bring physical risks. In a 1997 tragedy, thirty-one children were killed and fifty seriously injured when the truck they were riding in overturned. Authorities learned that the driver had left the main road, hoping to save time getting the workers to the fields by cutting through a cotton field. The truck plunged off the path into a canal filled with six feet of water.

One man who lost two children in the accident grieved, but said that the accident would not keep people from sending their children to work in the cotton fields. Parents were keeping their children home for a little while, he acknowledged, but they could not stop working for long. "Someday the children will have to go back to the fields," he said. "It will be against our will. But it will be a matter of necessity." His wife, however, did not agree. In her mind, no economic gain was worth the risk of any more of her children dying. "We are going to eat dust," she said bitterly, "or go begging in the streets. I will not send them. What has happened has burned our hearts."[81]

Human rights workers, concerned about the dangers to children working in this occupation, have asked why Egyptian cotton cannot be picked by machine, as it is in other countries. Officials in the Agriculture Ministry say that they have experimented with machines, but the fields in the Nile Delta are so densely planted that using machines would be a problem. The short answer, they say, is that children are necessary to the industry, and government ministers bristle at the idea that working is a punishment for children. "There is serious unemployment in this country," says one official. "We are not torturing these children, we are giving them jobs."[82]

Not Enough Room in Schools

Jordan and Yemen have many child laborers, too. The story is similar: There is a great deal of poverty, yet there are plenty of jobs for unskilled and semi-skilled workers. In Yemen, some children work in fields, but a great many more are peddlers on the street, restaurant workers, and car washers.

Unlike children in Egypt, who have access to schools but do not attend, only a very small minority of children in Yemen and Jordan have access to any schooling beyond kindergarten. Even in the cities, schools are underfunded and woefully understaffed. Faced with attending a school where one teacher reigns over a classroom of fifty or sixty children, it is not surprising that many prefer work.

Experts warn that children's lack of education will just make the problem worse. Illiterate children will never be able to get good, well-paying jobs. Today, 97 percent of working children come from families where parents can neither read nor write, and that cycle will continue unless school becomes a priority. But because of the widespread poverty, another income—even a small one—seems far more important than education.

In both Jordan and Yemen, it is technically illegal for children to hold jobs. In Jordan, the government has initiated a Child Labor Unit whose employees are supposed to investigate businesses that hire children. Ironically, these workers find that they are torn between reporting the children and keeping their secret. They say that they feel sympathy for the families who have so little to eat, and often fail to report child labor, even though it is against the law.

"The Problem Is Greed"

No country in the Middle East has more children working full-time than Pakistan. Human rights workers estimated in 2002 that more than 12 million Pakistani children work. In fact, one-fourth of Pakistan's workforce is made up of children, half of whom are under the age of ten.

Pakistan's birthrate is one of the highest in the world, and like Yemen and Jordan, it lacks enough schools to handle more than a third of its children. Unlike those countries, however, its ruling class has made no attempt to abolish child labor. In fact, even though there are existing laws that prohibit children from working full-time jobs, the government refuses to enforce them. Human rights workers insist that the government listens only to the wealthy, who make money by relying on a workforce that works for only one-third of what adults are paid for the same job.

"Inaction speaks louder than words," says the director of the Human Rights Commission of Pakistan. "This government is in continuous violation [of

A Land Run by Children

In his February 1996 article for the Atlantic Monthly, *Jonathan Silvers describes his visit to rural Pakistan, noting that nothing prepared him for the number of children working a variety of full-time jobs.*

To leave Lahore, the nation's intellectual and commercial center, is to enter a land populated and run by children. The change is as abrupt as it is extreme. The roads just beyond the city limits are congested with donkey carts, all of them driven by teamsters of eight or nine. Boys seem to have a monopoly on roadside attractions: gas stations, auto-repair centers, restaurants. When I pull into the Star Petroleum station . . . five miles from Lahore, three boys rush out of the garage to service my car. They are twelve, eight, and seven, and wear uniforms intended for men twice their size. The eldest has rolled up his pants and sleeves, but his colleagues helplessly trail theirs in the dirt. While the older boys fill my tank with a rusted hand pump, the youngest climbs onto the hood and cleans the windshield with a dangling sleeve. When I pull away, the boys rush back to the garage and to a diesel engine they are attempting to rebuild between fill-ups. No adults are visible on the premises.

UN agreements on the rights of children] and it has consistently refused to enforce those very laws it enacted to protect its most vulnerable citizens. . . . The problem is lack of political will. The problem is greed."[83]

Child labor in Pakistan is prevalent in both rural and urban areas. One visitor to the countryside found that a large portion of Pakistan's farmland was worked by children. In the poorest regions, yoked teams of three-, four-, and five-year-olds plow, seed, and harvest fields, working from dawn until dusk. "Children are cheaper to run than tractors," says one farmer, "and smarter than oxen."[84]

In the city children work in auto repair shops, brick factories, steel mills, and stone-crushing plants—at all hours of the day and night. They work with very little supervision from adults. There is an overseer who circulates around the factory or shop only to make sure that the jobs are being done correctly.

One business owner says that he would much rather employ children than adults. "[Children] make ideal employees," he says. "Boys at this stage of development [six or seven] are at the peak of their dexterity and endurance, and they're wonderfully obedient—they'd work around the clock if I asked them."[85]

The *Peshgi* System

One of the aspects of Pakistan's child labor situation that is most disturbing to human rights workers is *peshgi*, the system of indenturing children. There are many Pakistanis who are too poor to keep their children, and in return for a price, these parents may hand them over to a "master" who will train and employ them. The price, or *peshgi*, is paid to the parents in installments.

Writer Jonathan Silvers witnessed such a transaction while in the village of Wasan Pura. Sadique, a carpet manufacturer, was talking to Mirza, a brick maker who works as many as eighty hours per week but cannot afford to feed his children. Mirza brought his seven-year-old son, Nadeem, to Sadique, hoping the manufacturer would in effect, rent him. Sadique offered 5,000 rupees, which is the equivalent of $146, for the use of the boy. In return, Nadeem will work as a carpet weaver—without further pay—for five years.

The sum, which will be paid in several installments, is appallingly small, and will shrink as Sadique deducts Nadeem's food, materials, and tools. The master will also deduct money for mistakes the boy makes as he learns to weave carpets. In truth, Silvers learns, Pakistani parents consider themselves lucky if at the end of their child's service they are paid one-third of the *peshgi*.

While the parent receiving the *peshgi* is almost always shortchanged, the master makes a great deal of money, especially in Pakistan's large carpet industry. Such handwoven carpets are actually made of more than 7 million little knots of various colors. Pakistani carpet makers employ between six hundred thousand and 1 million children between the ages of four and fourteen

Indentured Pakistani children mold bricks at a brickyard. Many poor Pakistani families are forced to indenture their children in exchange for a small sum of money.

in their factories—roughly 90 percent of the carpet-making workforce. Factory owners say that the main reason is that children are cheap. For what an owner would pay one adult, he can hire three or four boys to do his weaving.

Turkey, Iran, and other nations where these carpets are made must charge more for them, since they have laws against child labor. That means that Turkey and Iran must pay adult wages for the work; this makes the carpets more expensive, but they are made without exploiting children. In contrast, since its rugs are so much cheaper, Pakistan's carpet exports have tripled since the 1970s. As a result

A young Pakistanti carpet weaver works at a loom. Although the parents of indentured children are paid very little, the employers profit handsomely from the child labor.

of that increased business, more factories have been opened throughout the country, with demand for more and more children at the looms.

"Your Boy Now Belongs to Me"

In addition to the unfair amount of money given to parents, the *peshgi* system is emotionally very difficult for many children. "It's not hard to imagine how hard it is for these kids," says one human rights worker. "They're basically being told to make their own way in the world when they should be home with their families. These are kids five, six, seven years old, and they're being asked to shoulder responsibilities many adults would find daunting."[86]

The masters are very clear about the chain of command when finalizing the deals with parents. Child workers are not allowed to return home—even in cases of emergency, such as a death in the family. They have no contact with their parents or siblings and are expected to work as many hours as the master dictates.

"Your boy now belongs to me," said one shop owner to the father of a small boy. "Please understand that so long as he works under my roof he is answerable only to me. Inform him that the needs of my shop take priority over those of his family, and [he] must do all he can to please me. If he does not, we will all be disappointed, him most of all."[87]

Punishments

Added to the stress of being away from home and family, child workers must often endure unfair treatment—including physical abuse—at the hands of their supervisors. One twelve-year-old girl who worked at a carpet loom said that the master considered her and her fellow workers commodities. Children were bought, sold, and traded, she says, as though they were cattle—and often were sold or traded to new masters whose factories were hundreds of miles from where they were originally bonded.

"The boys were beaten frequently to make them work long hours," she says. "The girls were often [sexually] violated. My best friend got ill after she was raped, and when she couldn't work, the master sold her to a friend of his in a village a thousand kilometers [620 miles] away. Her family was never told where she was sent, and they never saw her again."[88]

It is the same in other factories, such as those where Pakistani children sew soccer balls. Because child rights activists have attempted to document the horrid conditions of the factories by taking photographs, owners keep the lighting poor. They also prohibit the children—most between the ages of five and ten—from talking while they work. Those who fall asleep in the near-darkened room, or who whisper to a friend nearby, are taken to a shed and hung upside down by their knees. Repeat offenders are hit with a cane or are starved.

"At the Time, Work Seemed Glamorous"

In their interviews with children working full-time jobs, human rights workers have been surprised that many of them do not feel cheated or exploited.

In fact, some children say that they were excited about turning six or seven so that they could go to work. Many consider it a kind of milestone, a sign they are growing up.

One twelve-year-old girl who was "sold" to a brick maker under the *peshgi* system says she was more than ready to take on a job. "My friends and I knew that sooner or later we'd be sent off to the factories or the fields. We were tired of doing chores and minding infants," she says. "We looked forward to the day when we'd be given responsibilities and the chance to earn money. At the time, work seemed glamorous and children who worked quite important."[89]

Many parents also felt that it was not a bad thing for their young children to begin work. One mother of three says that she talked it over with her children when they were quite small. "When my children were three," she recalls, "I told them that they must be prepared to work for the good of the family. I told them again and again that they would be bonded at five. And when the time came for them to go, they were prepared and went without complaint."[90]

Jobs After Saddam

The years of Saddam Hussein's administration were marked by rampant unemployment and poverty, and as a result, Iraq has had its own large population of child laborers. Following the U.S.-led attack on Iraq in March 2003, the situation has not improved, but the jobs children hold are different.

These days, many Iraqi children make money by selling pieces of dis-carded metal from ammunition and abandoned planes and tanks they find. Karar, a nine-year-old who lives in Baghdad, works nine hours each day, squatting next to a large mound of discarded ammunition with a group of other children. Karar chips away at each bullet until he separates the copper casing from the bullet, and puts the copper chip into a bag.

Because of the junk left after the invasion, there is a great deal of metal to be salvaged. Experts say that there are perhaps a half-million spent shells from Iraqi army camps, as well as other scrap metal. A large sack full of copper chips earns a child about $1.90. With money to be made, thousands of children have eagerly joined in. "I can fill half a sack if I stay here for a long day," says Karar. "My mother says this is a good job. I give her my earnings."[91]

Kids As Soldiers

Not all of the violations of children's human rights involve them working. In fact, one of the most dangerous situations is using children as soldiers, and that is happening with increasing frequency in the Middle East. In Afghanistan, recent fighting between Taliban forces and rebels involved many young boys.

One fifteen-year-old, Mukhtar, had been fighting in the infantry of Afghanistan's army since he was eleven years old. His parents and siblings were killed by the Taliban then, and he joined the army to avenge their deaths. His platoon leader is proud of Mukhtar, bragging that the boy can shoot a man

Refugees at Work

In his article for the Baltimore Sun, *John Murphy describes how the lives of many Afghani children have changed when war has forced them to flee their homeland. As if the displacement were not enough, the inability of their parents to earn enough money as refugees has meant that many children have had to find jobs, too.*

When the first fingers of sunlight reach over the jagged mountains that surround this desert city [in Pakistan], Nissar Ahmad arrives at a tiny bakeshop to begin another day of work. He lights a fire in the giant brick oven. He cleans the baking trays. He squats beside the fire, using a long iron rod to pull the trays of biscuits from the oven.

Under the desert sun, the little shop heats up like a furnace. Nissar will work twelve hours before the day is over. For six days of work, he will earn 72 cents, enough to buy a liter of mineral water here. Nissar is seven years old.

He is also an Afghan refugee. And like many of the refugee children in this city near the Afghanistan border, he doesn't attend school. He can't read or write, add or subtract. But he has learned the lesson that life doesn't get any easier once you cross the border into Pakistan. . . .

Here, many refugee families are so poor that they must send their children to work. Afghan children who would not be old enough for kindergarten in the United States labor longer hours than most adults do.

Displaced Afghani refugee children like these kids making a rug often find work to help support their families.

in the beard at two hundred meters or point out camouflaged Taliban bunkers even through swirling sand.

Mukhtar's story is not unusual. Afghanistan, after all, has not seen peace in decades, so the children today have known nothing except violence. A reporter visiting Afghanistan in 2001 noted that children toting firearms was such a common sight that, "after a while, scenes of 12-year-olds skipping along with Kalashnikovs [Russian-made weapons] slung over their shoulders seems almost normal."[92]

"How Can We Convince Them"

Many children's rights advocates are deeply concerned by the nonchalance children in Afghanistan demonstrate toward killing. "One of the most difficult things to change in our country is the younger generation's mind-set," says one advocate. "How can we convince them that this thing called peace is better than the guns that they carry everywhere?"[93]

One of the problems, they say, is that children receive mixed messages about violence from many adults. While some try to explain that violence only leads to more death and more anger, others—especially military leaders—welcome the enthusiasm of the child soldiers.

The Taliban welcomed children into its armies as well. Many boys as young as ten or eleven were taken from refugee camps in Afghanistan and trained to use weapons. War orphans were also valuable to the Taliban. They made excellent soldiers since they had no homes to escape to. "Children are innocent," said one Taliban soldier, "so they are the best tools against the dark forces."[94]

What startles many human rights workers is how single-minded many Afghani children have become about the direction their lives have taken—especially those whose parents or other family members have been killed in war. These children are proud to have a mission, and are eager for vengeance. One insists that the rest of his life was set in motion when his parents were killed, and that he will spend the rest of his life pursuing the Taliban. Another says that he feels like a man when he fights for his people.

Ten-year-old Najibullah, who wants more than anything to learn to operate a rocket-propelled grenade launcher, says that he can hardly wait to grow. "I am small now," he says. "But I will be big when I shoot the Taliban who killed my aunt and uncle." As for the risk that he faces by being a soldier, Najibullah is not concerned. "If I am murdered by the Taliban," he shrugs, "then my sons will honor my name by killing the enemy."[95]

"I Hope . . . to Explode Myself"

If the dedication to vengeance among some Afghani children is discouraging for child advocates, then the dream of some children in the Palestinian territories to become suicide bombers is mind-boggling. "I hope to be a martyr," says twelve-year-old Ali, wearing a pretend dynamite-laden belt made of wood, wire, and electrical tape. "I hope

Both the Taliban and rebel forces conscripted many children, some as young as ten, into their armies.

"Sacrifice Is the Highest Honor"

The bitter conflict between Palestinians and Israelis is especially evident in the Gaza Strip. In her 2003 article "Why Palestinian Children Die," Maya Alleruzzo describes a protest march by Palestinians in the area and the role of some of their children.

Little Ali, masked in a kaffiyeh [Muslim head scarf] and carrying a toy gun made of pipes, marched earlier today in a demonstration marking Al Nakba or "the catastrophe," as Palestinians refer to the day Israel was founded in 1948. Given Abu Ali's start in life, his future might seem inevitable. Walking through the streets of Gaza City, one can see young boys playing with toy Kalashnikovs [weapons] and slingshots beneath the walls painted with graffiti depicting masked Hamas [Islamic terrorist] fighters, grenades, exploding buses. . . . If jobs here [for Palestinians] are scarce, there is one man [the funeral director] who is making enough to support his family.

Now, about 70 percent of his business comes from these large, loving tributes to the young fighters. Funeral marches are a citywide event. Young boys march—usually five kilometers from the hospital to the graveyard—alongside men shooting live rounds into the air.

Hisham Zaqout, whose nephew Youssef, 15, was killed when he tried to infiltrate an Israeli settlement, say the well-wishers, posters, and artistic tributes have helped ease the family's pain. "In Islam, sacrifice is the highest honor," he says. "Youssef did this for all of us to be free." The irony of his words is that the continued bombings and Israeli responses to them only continues the cycle of violence.

when I get [to be] 14 or 15 to explode myself."[96]

Human rights workers say that increasing numbers of Palestinian children are being taught that it is their patriotic duty to become human bombs as a way of avenging what they see as an unfair seizure of their land by the Israelis. They are taught that suicide bombing is the best way to frighten Israel's people, and that they have the right to do it.

Suicide bombing is taught by Islamic terrorist groups to boys between the ages of twelve and fifteen years old. Not only do they learn the fundamentals of explosives, but they are taught that to die is a great honor. They are shown pictures of young boys who have already died as martyrs, and are told that if they themselves are successful, they will be guaranteed a place in heaven. Explains one terror school teacher, "We are teaching them that after the suicide attacks, the man who makes it goes to the highest state in paradise."[97]

Surprisingly, instead of being horrified that their little boys are anxious to become martyrs, some Palestinian mothers applaud them. "I encourage him," says one mother of six, "and he should do this. God gave him to me to defend our land. Palestinian women must have more and more children till we liberate our land. This is a holy duty for all Palestinian people."[98]

However, many people—Palestinians and Israelis alike—worry about what the bitter language and escalating violence in the region are teaching their children. It is one thing, they say, when children want to participate in something their parents feel strongly about. It is natural, too, for many young people to adopt the political feelings of their parents, especially in a region of the Middle East that has seen so much turmoil.

But to present suicide as an option for their children is as appalling to many Palestinian parents as it is to Israeli parents. "It's sad," says one Palestinian woman. "It's no good to teach hate, let alone wish your children to die." Although she understands why Palestinians are angry with Israel, she stresses that she could never condone such violence against them. "How can any mother feel such [a] thing?" she wonders aloud. "How can she say she loves her sons when she tells them how proud they will make her when they die like that?"[99]

CHAPTER 5

Persecution of Minorities

Throughout the Middle East, groups of citizens are discriminated against by the government. In some cases, it is because they are different ethnically from the majority. In other cases, it is because they follow a different religion. The discrimination ranges in severity. Persecution can be subtle—such as a police force that is more likely to arrest minority citizens than those of the majority—or obviously brutal, such as a government that systematically uses military force to wipe out certain minority groups.

The Copts
One group that has been the object of ongoing persecution is the Coptic Christians, often referred to as Copts. In Egypt, Copts number about 7 million, a little more than 10 percent of the population. For many years, Copts and Muslims existed fairly easily together; however, since the 1990s the nation has become more conservative and the Copts have been an easy target for Muslim extremists.

Sometimes the persecution is subtle. The government simply looks the other way when Copts are mistreated. For example, many Copts have been forced to pay a form of protection money, called *gizia*, to certain Muslim groups. If a payment is late, or if a Copt refuses to pay it, he is beaten or killed. Copt shopkeepers have often been told they had to pay or their businesses would be burned.

An Egyptian bishop says that such extortion has been used on every Christian in his village, whenever there is an exchange of money, or when business is done. Whenever a Copt buys or sells goods, or harvests his land, a Muslim arrives to collect his share. "It's a system that has destroyed development," he insists. "It is a Mafia [system]."[100]

Asked whether the police know about what is happening, villagers nod affirmatively. The militants have complete freedom to impose the *gizia*, they say, even though the authorities are well acquainted with the men who demand the payments. "Everyone knows, the police know and do nothing," says one Copt villager. "I am very sad, because a lot of people are leaving because the situation is not sound."[101]

Egypt's Copts have been the target of violent attacks, too. In 1997, Muslim extremists stormed into one Copt church where a youth meeting was taking place, firing guns. Eleven young

Coptic priests give the Eucharist to an infant during mass. Since the 1990s, Coptic Christians have become targets of persecution at the hands of Muslim extremists.

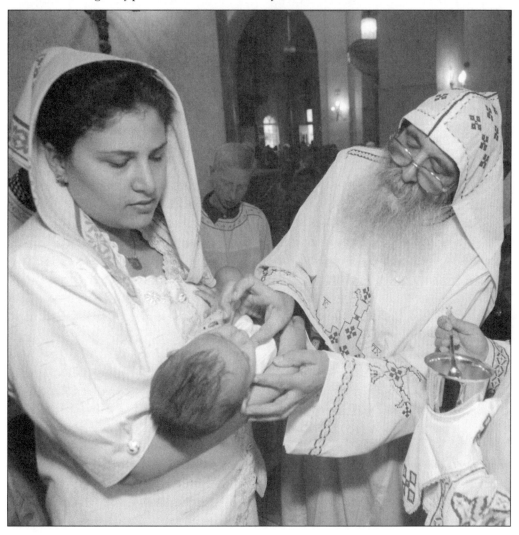

people were killed and five were wounded in what a government official called "a cowardly attack on the country's stability, security, and national unity."[102]

Nevertheless, such attacks on Copts have increased over the years, and although the Egyptian government officially condemned the violence, little has been done to prevent it. In an editorial printed in the *Middle East Times*, one observer noted that the government "has been so irresponsible on this issue that Copts fear approaching the police for assistance and protection because they see the largely Muslim police forces of Egypt clandestinely approving of the situation through their failure to address a situation that they know exists and know how to solve."[103]

Since the late 1990s, the discrimination against Coptic Christians has lessened somewhat. Even so, notes one Coptic bishop, the times are nervous ones for his people, for there are more subtle ways Copts are being persecuted. "We are living under huge social pressures," he says, "pushing Christians to [exile] status, and causing some faithful to become Muslims, especially for financial reasons. If you want a home or a job, undoubtedly you will be better looked at if you are Muslim."[104]

Being Muslim Is Not Enough
However, being Muslim in the Middle East is no guarantee that one will not be persecuted. In fact, some of the most widespread and violent cases of persecution are launched against Muslims by other Muslims. The reason for this is the mutual distrust and hostility between two Muslim groups—the Shiites and the Sunnis.

The antagonism between Shiites and Sunnis goes back to ancient times. When the prophet Muhammad died in 632, a huge power struggle erupted, for Muhammad had left no instructions about who should take over the leadership of Islam, a position that involved political, religious, and even military decision making.

Some of Muhammad's followers believed that the new leader should be someone related to the Prophet, while others believed that the elders of the community should choose the wisest and strongest Muslim to be his successor. Each group passionately felt that they were right, and the difference of opinion divided the followers of Islam. Some followed a blood relative of Muhammad, and they became known as the Shiites. Those who followed a leader chosen by the elders, meanwhile, were known as the Sunnis.

The differences between the two sects were more than philosophical. Wars between the two were fought throughout the Middle East, and most of the Shiites were ultimately driven from Saudi Arabia into what are now the nations of Iran and Iraq. Today, those are the only nations with a Shiite majority; Sunni Muslims outnumber Shiites in the rest of the region. And while they share some identical beliefs regarding the ideas of their Islamic faith, many Sunnis and Shiites differ on others. As a result, they continue to dislike and distrust one another.

"A Witness to My Murder Wouldn't Say Anything"

In an April 1997 article for the Middle East Times, *reporter Richard Engel interviewed a Coptic Christian in Egypt who explained how he is being forced to pay Muslim militants extortion money.*

Samir is planning to escape with his family from a small village near Abu Qurqas to Cairo. He fears for his life and has been told that if he refuses to pay *gizia* ("requital") money that Muslim villagers demand for "protection" of his family, he will be killed.

"They take whenever they need," says Samir, who was afraid to give his full name. "When they need weapons they take from the Christians. I'm scared I will be killed. Even if I was killed, no one would say anything. Even a witness to my murder wouldn't say anything."

Samir complains that *gizia* is increasing in a number of small villages in Upper Egypt, making it impossible to remain in the region.

"Everyone pays, but what can we do? There are so many people who deny it. They are lying! Everyone pays! I have no outlet!" says Samir, apologizing for his excitement.

Amgad, also from a village near Abu Qurqas, has been living in hiding in a poor district of Cairo for over a year. . . . He received three letters demanding *gizia* from the Gamma Islamiya, Egypt's largest Muslim militant group. The third letter . . . said, "We demand 10,000 (Egyptian pounds) from you tomorrow. . . . If you can't bring it [by then] . . . we will not accept even millions of pounds from you and you know the punishment for that. This is a final decision."

Discrimination in Saudi Arabia

In Saudi Arabia, the kingdom's Sunni leaders follow a very conservative type of Islam called Wahhabism, which is even more anti-Shiite than other Sunni sects. Because Saudi religious leaders share power with the royal family, there is a great deal of discrimination against the 2 million Shiites who live there.

"They view Shiites as deviants who must be steered to the official faith," explains one expert, "a purist [and extremely conservative] branch of Sunni Islam known as Wahhabism. . . . [Shiites] are shut out of sensitive government jobs, their religious books are banned, and many of their millennium-old ceremonies are prohibited."[105]

The Saudi government presents very different ideas about its attitude toward the Shiite population in their midst. The official viewpoint, expressed by the kingdom's deputy minister for Islamic affairs, is that there is no inequality. "There is no discrimination against the Shiites," he

Hazara men inspect a grave containing the remains of people executed by the Taliban. As Sunni Muslims, the Taliban launched an offensive against all Shiites, including the Hazaras.

says. "They are Muslims and citizens of Saudi Arabia. Discrimination in Saudi Arabia was not acceptable from the establishment of the state and until today."[106]

But examples of persecution and discrimination are widespread. Books about Islam that are distributed by the Saudi government advise against showing charity to even the poorest Shiites, and sharing food Shiites prepare. In Saudi schools, children are taught by Wahhabi clerics who make no secret of their disdain of Shiites. Asked whether it would make more sense to treat the Shiites better, if only for the sake of national unity, one cleric scoffed. "The Shiites?" he exclaimed. "They are the enemy number one."[107]

Though examples of physical violence against Shiites are rare in Saudi Arabia, many Shiites say they are angered by the constant exclusion from mainstream society, as well as the lack of equal rights. One Shiite businessman says that any time he visits the municipal courts to get permits or to fill out forms, the judges simply refuse to acknowledge his presence. And an editor is prohibited from having his magazine printed in Saudi Arabia because he is a Shiite. He therefore must pay more to have it printed in Lebanon and then smuggle it back to his Shiite Saudi subscribers.

Saudi Arabia's Shiite population has little hope that things will change, especially since the nation seems to be getting more conservative each year. Even so, they say they are tired of being treated like second-class citizens. Says one man flatly, "We've had enough of discrimination."[108]

Killing Shiites

In recent years, Shiites in Afghanistan have experienced not only discrimination but violence at the hands of the Taliban. The Taliban, like the Saudi religious leaders, had been schooled in conservative Sunni Wahhabism. As the Taliban encountered other Sunni people in southern and central Afghanistan, its goal was to subdue them. Taliban "advance" teams preceded the army in Afghan towns to encourage the citizens to cooperate with the invaders.

When the Taliban moved north, into lands held by Shiites, the goal was far more sinister. North of the capital city of Kabul, in the small villages of the Shomali plain, Taliban forces sent no advance teams. Instead, they unleashed bombing campaigns on the towns and villages, hoping to kill as many Shiites as possible.

The Hazaras, a group of Shiite Muslims distinctive because of their Asian features, were especially targeted. The Taliban stormed into their villages and went from house to house, rounding up all Hazara men and boys and executing them. One man who fled his village recalled that the killing was not cold and calculated but almost a frenzy. "They came and destroyed everything," he sobbed, "shooting and killing people—even donkeys—with knives and poking the eyes out of the people with steel rods." After killing as many people as they could, Taliban soldiers set fire to the homes, he said. "They did not leave a single house standing in my village."[109]

"They Tricked Us"

As word of the killings spread to other villages in northern Afghanistan, many people fled into the mountains to wait for the Taliban to leave. However, after a day or two, says one man, the Taliban announced a pardon for all villagers. They would not be harmed, said Taliban officials, and could come back to the village and harvest their crops.

The announcement was a lie. Within a few hours of returning to their fields, many of the Hazara men were seized by Taliban forces, handcuffed, and taken to the police station. From there they were loaded into a pickup truck and driven to a shallow pit and shot. "They tricked us," says one man who miraculously survived. "If we had known they would kill us, we would not have come."[110] He survived, he says, because one of the men shot by the Taliban fell on top of him and the soldiers assumed he was dead like the others.

In the town of Mazar-e Sharif, where several ethnic minorities live (including Hazaras), the worst killings occurred. Several thousand civilians were shot—many children as young as five or six. Women and girls in Hazara neighborhoods were kidnapped and raped by Taliban soldiers. Thousands of prisoners—many in their teens—were marched to the city jail and then loaded into large container trucks to be transported to other sites for execution. Some of those executions, however, were largely unnecessary, because hundreds of the prisoners died of heat stroke or asphyxiation in the crowded containers.

Human rights groups around the world condemned the action, saying that there was no doubt that the Taliban was committing acts of ethnic cleansing—killing off cultures and religious groups different from their own. Jawad, a Hazara political worker, says that everyone in the region knows that the spiritual leader of the Taliban, Mullah Omar, ordered the soldiers to kill all Hazaras. "He once made an infamous statement," says Jawad, "that all the Tajiks should go to Tajikistan, the Uzbeks to Uzbekistan, and the Hazara to Ghoristan—that is the word for 'cemetery.'"[111]

The Taliban soldiers did not keep the massacre at Mazar-e Sharif a secret. In fact, they were pleased at their successful killing of thousands of people. They erected a large sign at the site of one of the execution pits. "By God's grace," it says, "the Taliban captured the northern region of Afghanistan in 1998, and massacred the pagans."[112]

Shiites Under Saddam

Although Shiite Muslims outnumber the Sunnis in Iraq, power has been completely in the hands of the Sunnis. Saddam targeted the Shiites for persecution, just as the Taliban did, but for political rather than religious reasons. Saddam feared the Shiites because of their numbers and because he worried that if a strong leader rose up among them, the Shiites of Iraq could overwhelm the ruling Sunni minority.

His concern grew after the Shiites in neighboring Iran revolted against the shah and formed their own government headed by the Ayatollah Khomeini. Khomeini spoke out vehemently against Saddam and the Sunnis of Iraq, and urged Shiites in Iraq to rise up against them. When a Shiite extremist tried to assassinate one of Saddam's ministers, Saddam decided to begin a massive campaign against Shiite communities in Iraq.

Saddam's security guards rounded up Shiites by the thousands, throwing them into prisons and government interrogation centers. Were they working for the overthrow of the government? Did they know the names of any neighbors or family members who were working against Saddam? The questioning went on and on, and the interrogators often resorted to torture to get answers to their questions.

Saddam also promptly made membership in the Dawa Party, a Shiite political party, a crime punishable by death. Soldiers were instructed to go house to house looking for Dawa members, as well as Shiite religious leaders. Any they found were arrested and taken to a detention center.

It was not until after Saddam had fled Baghdad during the U.S. invasion in 2003 that the world truly understood the enormity of his crimes against the Shiites. It was then that people in towns such as Basra and Hilla, where many Shiites lived, began to gather at the sites of what they knew were communal graves. Many said that they thought Saddam was probably dead, or would be soon, and thus they felt brave enough to look for relatives and friends who had disappeared years ago.

Many of the graves held thousands of bodies, and experts claimed that there were hundreds of graves just like these scattered across Iraq. They all are believed to contain the remains of Shiites, as well as others who were threats to Saddam and who had been killed at his request.

As one reporter watched people combing through a communal grave, one man found his younger brother, identifying him by a swatch of clothing still attached to the bones. A woman nearby cried over the bodies of her sister and her two small children. Another man said he had to keep looking. "I've been here for six days," he said, "looking for two brothers and two sons. I do not know when I will stop."[113]

Continuing Anxiety

Even as post-Saddam Iraq tries to rebuild and fashion a new government, the Shiites still face difficulties. On March 2, 2004, which was Ashura, the holiest day of the Shiite calendar, three suicide bombers killed 70 people and injured 320 as they visited Kazimiyah Mosque.

Many Shiites believed that the attacks were an attempt to frighten them into taking a lesser role in Iraqi politics. However, when thousands of mourners took to the Baghdad streets the following day, there was no sense of fear. "These crowds are a show of defiance to those who carried out the attacks," declared one mourner. "The people want to show that they are not affected and that there will never be a . . . divide in Iraq."[114]

Shiite Muslims search a mass grave in Iraq for the remains of loved ones. During Saddam Hussein's reign, Shiites were targeted, terrorized, and murdered by the thousands.

Other Shiites were not sure what the effect of the bombings would be. They noted that violence against Shiites has increased in Pakistan, too. Gunmen in Quetta opened fire on a religious parade there, killing forty-four Shiites. Some expressed anxiety that the hostility Saddam had shown toward them was still alive in the world.

One Kuwaiti Shiite disagrees. He believes that the Shiite people throughout the Middle East have gained great strength since Saddam's presidency ended. "Before the fall of the Baathist regime in Iraq," he says, "governments here did not believe that Shiites could be powerful, but it's different now. Shiites are stronger."[115]

The Kurds

While Saddam attempted to hide the evidence of the genocide of the Shiite people of Iraq, he did not conceal any traces of the same policy waged against the Kurds. The Kurds are a non-Arab people who live in northern Iraq, Syria, Turkey, and parts of Iran. They had sought independence, but Saddam had refused to allow it. As Kurdish rebels staged demonstrations in protest, Saddam's security forces carried out mass arrests and executions.

He instructed Iraqi soldiers to not tolerate any Kurdish demonstrations, peaceful or otherwise. "Shoot at demonstrators," he ordered, "with the aim of killing 95 percent of them and saving the rest for interrogation."[116] In the late 1980s, Saddam ordered the execution of more than ten thousand Kurdish men and boys, and he had civilians from more than twelve thousand Kurdish villages relocated to concentration camps.

Saddam also authorized the use of chemical weapons against his own citizens. His cousin General Ali Hassan al-Majid was put in charge of the mission. Known by many as "Chemical Ali" because of his preference for gas and other nonconventional weapons, al-Majid dropped a lethal combination of nerve gas and mustard gas on a city in northeastern Iraq called Halabja in

March 1988. In one day, more than five thousand Kurds—many of them women and children—were killed by the poison gas.

Like the Shiites, the Kurds in post-Saddam Iraq are working hard to gain a voice in the new government. In March 2004, representatives signed an agreement that guaranteed Kurdish linguistic, cultural, and political rights in Iraq. "For the first time," said one Kurd in Baghdad happily, "I feel Iraqi."[117]

Kurds in Syria

In nearby Syria, the Kurdish population would like the same guarantees, but have had no success. Though they have not endured the mass executions and arrests that Iraqi Kurds under Saddam endured, they still face widespread dis-

A Kurdish woman recovers in a hospital after sustaining injuries during Saddam Hussein's 1988 nerve and mustard gas attack on the northeastern Iraqi city of Halabja.

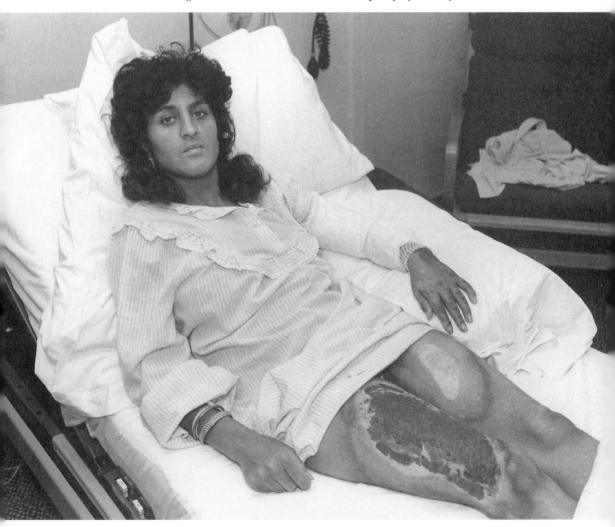

Syrian Kurds demonstrate after a 2004 police attack. Problems between Arabs and Kurds in Syria have been on the rise since the 1960s.

crimination. More than 10 percent of Syria's population is made up of Kurds, many of whom came to Syria decades ago to escape Turkish oppression. However, when they arrived the Kurds were considered illegal aliens by the Syrian government, and as such, they have been denied a number of opportunities afforded other Syrians. They were prohibited from becoming citizens, and from owning property. They could not send their children to public schools. They are also prohibited from speaking Kurdish in public and from teaching Kurdish customs to their children.

The problem began in 1962 when the Syrian Baath Party relocated more than 120,000 Kurds living near the Syria-Turkey border. The Baathists, who are pro-Arab, worried that the Syrian

Kurds were living in such close proximity to the Turkish Kurds that they might become too powerful.

To avoid such a situation, the Syrian government removed the Kurds from their land and relocated thousands of Arabs there instead. And while the Kurds had had no schools or other services, the new Arab settlements were provided with excellent schools, roads, and health clinics.

The Kurds, on the other hand, were stripped of their citizenship. With neither land nor rights, many Kurds drifted to Damascus or other Syrian cities, where they were forbidden to even speak the Kurdish language in public. The names of Kurdish villages and shops were changed to Arabic, and Kurdish parents were even urged to give their children Arabic names. Says one member of the Syrian Kurdish Democratic Party, "The authorities wanted to erase the Kurdish identity."[118]

"We Just Want Our Culture and Freedom"

Things have eased somewhat over the years. Kurdish people may legally speak their language. Occasionally, in fact, Kurdish singers perform on Syrian television. However, Kurds are still unable to become citizens and thus lack the benefits citizenship includes. They may not travel abroad, nor can they legally own businesses. Kurds in Syria tend to be far poorer than Syrian Arabs. And while they may speak Kurdish to one another, it is still forbidden to teach it in schools. Because of these injustices, Kurds have held protests in Damascus and other Syrian cities.

One member of the Syrian Kurdish Democratic Progressive Party said that

This photo shows a portion of the wall that separates Israel from the West Bank. Israelis contend that the barrier is necessary as a security measure against Palestinian suicide bombers.

the goals of Syrian Kurds are much less ambitious than those of Iraqi Kurds. "Their aim in Iraq is to get a state of their own," he explains. "But in Syria, we just want our culture and freedom as Syrian nationals."[119]

Another Kurdish reformer says that the human rights violations need to be corrected for Kurds to be accepted as important members of Syrian society: "We must remove the barriers imposed on the Kurdish language and culture and recognize the existence of the Kurdish nationality within the unity of the country. Our people have endured sufferings and poverty because of this policy of discrimination that has been imposed for several decades."[120]

Discrimination or Protection?

While the discrimination against the Kurds has been clearly evident, there are some situations in the Middle East where sides disagree over whether discrimination has really occurred. In the area of Israel known as the West Bank, which is the site of a great deal of violence between Israelis and Palestinians, the topics of discrimination and persecution provoke much controversy.

One example is a three-hundred-mile-long barrier—a series of walls, fences, and razor wire—that Israel began building in 2003. Israeli officials say that the barrier is being constructed to protect Israel from suicide bombers who originate in Palestinian settlements and who target Israeli citizens. Some insist that killing innocent civilians is the extreme violation of human rights. Why, they wonder, should Israel have to jus-

tify the construction of a wall to protect its citizens from terrorists?

One woman whose husband was killed in a suicide bombing was adamant that the wall was necessary. In a newspaper article about the barrier, she insisted that had the barrier existed a few weeks before, she would not be a widow today. "I am appealing to you," she explained in the article, which detailed the pros and cons of the barrier, "as someone . . . whose tragedy could have been averted by the separation fence."[121]

But to Palestinians, the barrier is seen as an Israeli trick to take over more land, land that, they say, belongs to Palestinians. Many say that they sympathize with the need for security against suicide bombers. "If Israel says this is about security, we understand that," says one Palestinian man. However, he says, that does not justify the government's building the barrier on their land. "It doesn't explain why the wall is being built where it's being built," he says, "and how it's being built. The real strategy behind the wall is to take as much land as possible while maximizing the number of Palestinians on the other side. It's a land grab."[122]

The daily lives of many Palestinians are affected by the new barrier. A UN study in November 2003 found that about 400,000 Palestinians would be separated from jobs, schools, and hospitals. Some farmers are angry that the plan puts them on one side of the barrier and their fields on the other.

Residents in one village, Sheik Saad, are worried about what the barrier will

Angry Palestinians demonstrate against the security wall in 2003. Many Palestinians feel that the wall makes them prisoners in their own homes.

do to them. In March 2004, the government bulldozed the road leading out of their village to begin construction of that section of the wall. Large mounds of concrete blocks and dirt prevented travel to Jerusalem, where many of the residents work. Some continued to go to work by climbing over the hills, but they knew that would not be possible once the wall was completed.

One elderly woman was sad because her children and their families lived on one side of the barrier while she was on the other. A new father was angry because he could not even get to a store. "We're cut off from everything and everyone," he said. "We're prisoners in

our own homes. I can't even buy baby formula for my twins. How does anyone expect us to live like this?"[123]

Many human rights workers around the world—including Israeli ones—are sympathetic. They say that the barrier will definitely be unfair to many Palestinians. Besides the inconvenience and separation from jobs and family members, human rights experts believe that the barrier sends a strong message that Palestinians' rights are not respected. "This is quite the extreme example of the negative human rights impact of the barrier," says a researcher with an Israeli human rights group called B'tselem. "They will have to live in a cage or leave."[124]

When?

Regardless of whether human rights violations are easily recognized or not, the nations of the Middle East have a great deal of work to do if conditions are to improve for their citizens. Some human rights workers worry that the harmful traditions of government repression, discrimination against women, and hatreds of certain ethnic and religious groups are too ingrained to be eliminated. Others, however, would like to believe there is reason for optimism.

"The idea that knowledge is power is right," says Rob, a human rights advocate. "Today more than ever before people are realizing they are not alone. The Internet helps, as does an expanding human rights community. Even in some of the most remote areas, word gets out to people who care, and there are many throughout the world."[125]

Meanwhile, to the three-year-old yoked to a plow in Pakistan, the woman in Kuwait who is not permitted to vote, the reporters held without bail in Saudi prisons, or any of the millions suffering abuse of basic human rights, the future simply cannot come fast enough.

NOTES

Chapter 1:
Systems of Injustice

1. Theo Nichols, telephone interview with author, January 29, 2004.
2. Quoted in Mansour Farhang, "Spies Under the Persian Rug," *Nation*, June 26, 2000, p. 31.
3. Quoted in Farhang, "Spies Under the Persian Rug," p. 31.
4. Quoted in *BBC Monitoring Middle East*, "Released Cleric Describes Detention Conditions," May 7, 2002, p. 1.
5. Farhang, "Spies Under the Persian Rug," p. 31.
6. Mohammad Hajizadeh, "Commentary Views State of Prisons," Asia Africa Intelligence Wire, November 5, 2003, n.p.
7. *Human Rights Watch World Report 2003*, "Iran," www.hrw.org/wr2k3/mideast3.html.
8. Quoted in Susan Sachs, "Project: Open Book—Saudi Arabia," March 28, 2000. www.domini.org/openbook/sau20000328.html.
9. Quoted in Amnesty International, "Saudi Arabia Remains Fertile Ground for Torture with Impunity," May 2002. www.amnesty.org/library/index/ENGMDE2230042002.htm.
10. Quoted in Amnesty International, "Saudi Arabia Remains Fertile Ground."
11. Quoted in Margarette Driscoll, "Saudis Sentenced Me to Crucifixion, Says Freed Scot," *Sunday Times* (London). September 7, 2003, p. 1.
12. Quoted in Amnesty International, "Saudi Arabia Remains Fertile Ground."
13. Quoted in Amnesty International Canada, "Saudi Arabia: End Secrecy, End Suffering," 2000. www.amnesty.ca/SaudiArabia/1htm.
14. Quoted in Robert Fisk, "Women Beheaded in Saudi Execution Frenzy," *Independent* (London), July 23, 1999, p. 13.
15. Quoted in Amnesty International Canada, "Saudi Arabia."
16. Quoted in Driscoll, "Saudis Sentenced Me to Crucifixions," p. 1.
17. Quoted in Con Coughlin, *Saddam: King of Terror*. New York:

Ecco, 2002, p. 48.

18. Quoted in Adel Darwish and Gregory Alexander, *Unholy Babylon: The Secret History of Saddam's War*. New York: St. Martin's, 1991, p. 201.

19. Coughlin, *Saddam*, p. 161.

20. Quoted in Danny Kopp, "Extraordinary Measures Permitted," *Financial Times* (London), April 8, 2002, p. 6.

21. Quoted in Kopp, "Extraordinary Measures Permitted," p. 6.

22. Quoted in *BBC News*, "Campaigners Demand U.S. Torture Probe," December 27, 2002. http://news.bbc.co.uk/s/hi/americas/2607629.stm.

23. Quoted in *BBC News*, "Campaigners Demand U.S. Torture Probe."

24. Nichols, interview.

Chapter 2:
Women and Injustice

25. Quoted in Michael Lev, "Holy War Without End," *Chicago Tribune*, November 24, 1996, p. 1.

26. Quoted in *Sunday Mirror* (London), "The West at War," September 30, 2001, p. 8.

27. Quoted in *Greenboro News Record*, "Taliban 'Dress Code' Alters Women's Lives," October 30, 1996, p. A12.

28. Quoted in Rosemarie Skaine, *The Women of Afghanistan Under the Taliban*. Jefferson, NC: McFarland, 2002, p. 22.

29. Quoted in *Time*, "About Face," December 3, 2001, p. 34.

30. Quoted in Sajida Hayat, "Kabul: The City Where Even the Sunrise and Sunset Have Been Upset for a Long Time," Revolutionary Association of the Women of Afghanistan, January 2000. www.rawa.org/sajida.html.

31. Quoted in Skaine, *The Women of Afghanistan Under the Taliban*, p. 22.

32. Quoted in *Time*, "The Women of Islam," December 3, 2001, p. 50.

33. Nichols, interview.

34. Quoted in Colbert I. King, "Saudi Arabia's Apartheid," *Washington Post*, December 22, 2001, p. A23.

35. Nira, interview with author, Minneapolis, MN, February 26, 2004.

36. Quoted in Donna Abu-Nasr, "Religious Police Taking Their Toll on Saudi People," *Tulsa World*, April 28, 2002, p. 12.

37. Raid Qusti, "Our 'Female Problem,'" *Washington Post*, July 9, 2002, p. A21.

38. Quoted in Human Rights Watch, "Saudi Arabia: Religious Police Role in School Fire Criticized," March 15, 2002. www.hrw.org/press/2002/03/saudischool.htm.

39. Quoted in Mona Eltahawy, "They Died for Lack of a Head Scarf," *Washington Post*, March 19, 2002, p. A21.

40. Quoted in Human Rights Watch, "Saudi Arabia."

41. Qusti, "Our 'Female Problem,'" p. A21.

42. *The Koran*, 5th ed., trans. N.J. Dawood. Harmondsworth, NY: Penguin, 1990, ch. 4:34.

43. Quoted in Sally Armstrong, *Veiled Threat: The Hidden Power of the Women of Afghanistan*. New York: Four Walls Eight Windows, 2002, p. 102.

44. Quoted in Armstrong, *Veiled Threat*, p. 99.

45. Armstrong, *Veiled Threat*, p. 99.

46. Quoted in Armstrong, *Veiled Threat*, p. 98.

47. Nira, interview.

48. Quoted in Borzou Daragahi, "I Would Build Skyscrapers. I Have Real Dreams!" *Arizona Daily Star*, March 19, 2004. www.dailystar.com.

Chapter 3:
The Right of Expression

49. Ali, interview with author, Minneapolis, MN, February 27, 2004.

50. Quoted in Reporters Without Borders, "Censorship and Self-Censorship," April 2002. www.rsf.org/ print.php3?id-article=1436.

51. Quoted in Reporters without Borders, "Censorship and Self-Censorship."

52. Ali, interview.

53. Quoted in Reporters Without Borders, "Regime Jails Journalist for Eight Years and Suspends More Publications," July 2002. www.rsf.org/print.php3?id-article=2075.

54. Quoted in Fary Rosenblatt, "Between the Lines," *New York Jewish Week*, August 1, 2003, p. 7.

55. Quoted in Lawrence Wright, "Kingdom of Silence," *New Yorker*, January 5, 2004, p. 48.

56. Quoted in Wright, "Kingdom of Silence," p. 48.

57. Coughlin, *Saddam*, p. 170.

58. Quoted in Coughlin, *Saddam*, p. 172.

59. Quoted in Mohamed Khalifa, "Censorship Welcomed in Egypt," *Houston Chronicle*, October 12, 2003, p. 27.

60. Quoted in Khalifa, "Censorship Welcomed in Egypt," p. 27.

61. Quoted in Robin Wright, *The Last Great Revolution: Turmoil and Transformation in Iran*. New York: Alfred A. Knopf, 2000, p. 90.

62. Quoted in Wright, *The Last Great Revolution*, p. 90.

63. Azadeh Moaveni, "The Age of Googoosh," *Time Europe*, August 28, 2000. www.time.com/time/europe/webonly/mideast/2000/08/googoosh.html.

64. Quoted in Wright, *The Last Great Revolution*, p. 117.

65. Quoted in Nadya Labi, "Rhythmless Nation," *Time*, September 15, 2001, p. 60.

66. Quoted in Michael Lev, "Tyranny of Religion Imperils Rich Culture," *Chicago Tribune*, December 3, 1996, p. 1.

67. Quoted in Lev, "Tyranny of Religion," p. 1.

68. John Sifton, "A Last Road Trip Through Premodern Afghanistan," Peace Pledge Union, September 30, 2001. www.ppu.org.uk/temp/last-trip.html.

69. Quoted in Lev, "Tyranny of Religion," p. 1.

70. Wright, "Kingdom of Silence," p. 48.

71. Wright, "Kingdom of Silence," p. 48.
72. Quoted in Human Rights Watch, "The Internet in the Mideast and North Africa: Iraq," June 1999. www.hrw.org/advocacy/internet/mena/iraq.htm.
73. Quoted in Human Rights Watch, "The Internet in the Mideast and North Africa: Saudi Arabia," June 1999. www.hrw.org/advocacy/internet/mena/saudi.htm.
74. Quoted in Human Rights Watch, "The Internet in the Mideast and North Africa: Syria," June 1999. www.hrw.org/advocacy/internet/mena/syria.htm.
75. Quoted in Dave Montgomery, "Satellite Television Brings Outside World to Saudi Arabia," Knight Ridder/Tribune News Service, December 13, 2003, n.p.

Chapter 4: Children's Rights

76. Nichols, interview.
77. Nichols, interview.
78. Quoted in Emad Mekay, "An Economic Essential?" Middle East, November 1997, p. 38.
79. Quoted in Mekay, "An Economic Essential?" p. 38.
80. Quoted in Mekay, "An Economic Essential?" p. 38.
81. Quoted in Douglas Jehl, "King Cotton Exacts a Tragic Toll from the Young," New York Times, September 25, 1997, p. A4.
82. Quoted in Mekay, "An Economic Essential?" p. 38.
83. Quoted in Jonathan Silvers, "Child Labor in Pakistan," Atlantic Monthly, February 1996. www.theatlantic.com/issues/96feb/pakistan/pakistan.htm.
84. Quoted in Silvers, "Child Labor in Pakistan."
85. Quoted in Silvers, "Child Labor in Pakistan."
86. Nichols, interview.
87. Quoted in Silvers, "Child Labor in Pakistan."
88. Quoted in Silvers, "Child Labor in Pakistan."
89. Quoted in Silvers, "Child Labor in Pakistan."
90. Quoted in Silvers, "Child Labor in Pakistan."
91. Quoted in Vivienne Walt, "Iraqi Children Working to Survive with Their Parents Struggling," Boston Globe, August 12, 2003, p. A1.
92. Quoted in Time International, "The Child Soldiers," November 12, 2001, p. 50.
93. Quoted in Time International, "The Child Soldiers," p. 50.
94. Quoted in Time International, "The Child Soldiers," p. 50.
95. Quoted in Time International, "The Child Soldiers," p. 50.
96. Quoted in Maya Alleruzzo, "Why Palestinian Children Die," Betar-Tagar UK, July 30, 2003. www.betar.co.uk/articles/betar1059578683.php.
97. Quoted in Jeremy Cooke, "School Trains Suicide Bombers," BBC News, July 18, 2001. http://news.bbc.co.uk/1/hi/world/middle_east/1446003.stm.
98. Quoted in Alleruzzo, "Why Palestinian Children Die."
99. Nahla, interview with author,

South Saint Paul, MN, March 2, 2004.

Chapter 5:
Persecution of Minorities

100. Quoted in Richard Engel, "Fundamentalists Demand Mafia-Style Protection Money from Copts," *Middle East Times*, April 1997. www.metimes.com/cens/gizia.htm.

101. Quoted in Engel, "Fundamentalists Demand Mafia-Style Protection Money."

102. Quoted in U.S. Copts Home Page, "Three Slain After Egypt Church Massacre," February 1997. pweb.net com.com/~us_copts/news.htm.

103. Quoted in U.S. Copts Home Page, "Killing of Samir Wassef," June 1997. pweb.netcom.com/~us_copts/ news.htm.

104. Quoted in Giuseppe Caffulli, "An Interview with Cardinal Stephanos II Ghattas," *Asia News*, March 11, 2004, p. 16.

105. Yaroslav Trofimov, "Saudi Shiites See Gains from U.S. Invasion of Iraq," *Wall Street Journal*, February 3, 2003, p. 1.

106. Quoted in Trofimov, "Saudi Shiites See Gains," p. 1.

107. Quoted in Trofimov, "Saudi Shiites See Gains," p. 1.

108. Quoted in Trofimov, "Saudi Shiites See Gains," p. 1.

109. Quoted in Christina Lamb, "Taliban Brings Terror to Refugee Camps," *London Telegraph*, September 30, 2001. www.telegraph.co.uk.

110. Quoted in Carlotta Gall, "Killings from Taliban's Era Still Haunt a Valley," *New York Times*, July 25, 2002, p. A1.

111. Quoted in Gall, "Killings from Taliban's Era," p. A1.

112. Quoted in Dexter Filkins, "Under Autumn Snow, Footnotes to Village's Sorrowful Death," *New York Times*, December 9, 2001, p. B1.

113. Quoted in Patrick Healy, "Mourners Grieve at Mass Iraqi Grave," Knight-Ridder/Tribune Business News, May 15, 2003, n.p.

114. Quoted in *Jordan Times*, "Shiite Muslims in Baghdad Gather to Bury Their Dead After Suicide Bombings," March 4, 2004, p. 1.

115. Quoted in Vincent Vulin, "After Saddam, Shiites in Kuwait Becoming Vocal About Rights," *Gulf News Online*, March 12, 2004. www.gulf-news.com/Articles/news.asp?ArticleID=113538.

116. Quoted in Timothy Maier, "Horror Stories," *Insight on the News*, May 13, 2003, p. 18.

117. Quoted in Borzou Daragahi, "Kurds Say They Deserve More Rights, Land, Autonomy," *Washington Times*, March 15, 2004. www.washington times.com/world/20040315-100009-9985r.htm.

118. Quoted in Nicholas Blanford, "As War Looms, the Voice of Kurds Is Heard in Syria," *Christian Science Monitor*, November 20, 2002, p. 7.

119. Quoted in Blanford, "As War Looms," p. 7.

120. Quoted in *Kurdistan Observer*, "Kurds Protest Outside Syrian

Parliament Against Discrimination," December 10, 2002. www. konews/ 11-12-02-kurds-protest-outside-syrian-parli.htm.

121. Quoted in *BBC World News*, "World Court Examines Barrier Row," February 23, 2004. www. bbc.co.uk/2/hi/middle-east/ 3512255.stm.

122. Quoted in Ken Ellingwood, "Fence Alters Life for Arabs," *Detroit News*, February 23, 2004. www.det news.com/2004/nations/0402/ 23/a04_71662.htm.

123. Quoted in Lara Sukhtian, "West Bank Town's Plight Highlights Barrier's Impact," *Columbian*, March 2, 2004, p. A5.

124. Quoted in Sukhtian, "West Bank Town's Plight," p. A5.

125. Rob, interview with author, Minneapolis, MN, March 12, 2004.

FOR FURTHER READING

Books

Leila Merrell Foster, *Oman*. New York: Childrens Press, 1999. Helpful material on Islam in this nation, as well as the historical background of Oman's social system.

Miriam Greenblatt, *Iran*. New York: Childrens Press, 2003. Good information on the structure of the theocracy and the changes in the judicial system since the 1979 revolution.

David L. Parker, *Stolen Dreams: Portraits of Working Children*. Minneapolis: Lerner, 1998. Very readable book about bonded children, especially rug weavers in Pakistan. Great photographs.

Gail B. Stewart, *Life Under the Taliban*. San Diego: Lucent Books, 2004. Helpful information about the lack of woman's rights and the violation of rights of expression in Afghanistan during the Taliban's reign.

Web Sites

Human Rights Watch (www.hrw.org). Organized by topic as well as nation, this site offers up-to-the-minute news about violations of human rights around the world. Also includes suggested ways for people to express their concern over various topics, such as child labor and capital punishment.

Revolutionary Association of the Women of Afghanistan (www. rawa. org). This is the official Web site for women who have risked their lives to document human rights abuses in Afghanistan under the Taliban, especially the systematic abuse of women. There are warnings provided about particular pictures that may prove disturbing to some visitors.

WORKS CONSULTED

Books

Sally Armstrong, *Veiled Threat: The Hidden Power of the Women of Afghanistan*. New York: Four Walls Eight Windows, 2002. Very readable, with helpful information about various forms of persecution against Middle Eastern women.

Con Coughlin, *Saddam: King of Terror*. New York: Ecco, 2002. A challenging but fascinating book about the regime of Saddam Hussein. A great deal of background on human rights abuse allegations is provided.

Adel Darwish and Gregory Alexander, *Unholy Babylon: The Secret History of Saddam's War*. New York: St. Martin's, 1991. Good details about the purges of political enemies at the beginning of Saddam's regime.

The Koran. 5th ed. Trans. N.J. Dawood. Harmondsworth, NY: Penguin, 1990. This edition has an index and helpful explanatory notes.

Rosemarie Skaine, *The Women of Afghanistan Under the Taliban*. Jefferson, NC: McFarland, 2002. Excellent source with great bibliography and interviews with a number of women who survived the Taliban.

Robin Wright, *The Last Great Revolution: Turmoil and Transformation in Iran*. New York: Alfred A. Knopf, 2000. Helpful index and very informative chapter on movies and entertainment under religious scrutiny.

Periodicals

Donna Abu-Nasr, "Religious Police Taking Their Toll on Saudi People," *Tulsa World*, April 28, 2002.

BBC Monitoring Middle East, "Iraqi President Meets Artists, Discusses Censorship," November 2, 2002.

———, "Released Cleric Describes Detention Conditions," May 7, 2002.

Nicholas Blanford, "As War Looms, the Voice of Kurds Is Heard in Syria," *Christian Science Monitor*, November 20, 2002.

Giuseppe Caffulli, "An Interview with Cardinal Stephanos II Ghattas," *Asia News*, March 11, 2004.

Isobel Coleman, "Saudi Women Should Be Given Citizens' Rights," *Financial Times*, November 24, 2003.

Ali Daraghmeh, "Suicide Boys Shock Even Palestinians," *Pittsburgh Post-Gazette*, March 1, 2004.

Margarette Driscoll, "Saudis Sentenced

Me to Crucifixion, Says Freed Scot," *Sunday Times* (London), September 7, 2003.

Mona Eltahawy, "They Died for Lack of a Head Scarf," *Washington Post*, March 19, 2002.

Mansour Farhang, "Spies Under the Persian Rug," *Nation*, June 26, 2000.

Dexter Filkins, "Under Autumn Snow, Footnotes to Village's Sorrowful Death," *New York Times*, December 9, 2001.

Robert Fisk, "Women Beheaded in Saudi Execution Frenzy," *Independent* (London), July 23, 1999.

Carlotta Gall, "Killings from Taliban's Era Still Haunt a Valley," *New York Times*, July 25, 2002.

Greenboro News Record, "Taliban 'Dress Code' Alters Women's Lives," October 30, 1996.

Mohammad Hajizadeh, "Commentary Views State of Prisons," Asia Africa Intelligence Wire, November 5, 2003.

Patrick Healy, "Mourners Grieve at Mass Iraqi Grave," Knight-Ridder/Tribune Business News, May 15, 2003.

Japan Times, "Taliban Amputates Thief's Hand and Foot," June 21, 1998.

Douglas Jehl, "King Cotton Exacts a Tragic Toll from the Young," *New York Times*, September 25, 1997.

Jordan Times, "Shiite Muslims in Baghdad Gather to Bury Their Dead After Suicide Bombings," March 4, 2004.

Mohamed Khalifa, "Censorship Welcomed in Egypt," *Houston Chronicle*, October 12, 2003.

Colbert I. King, "Saudi Arabia's Apartheid," *Washington Post*, December 22, 2001.

Danny Kopp, "Extraordinary Measures Permitted," *Financial Times* (London), April 8, 2002.

Nadya Labi, "Rhythmless Nation," *Time*, September 15, 2001.

Michael Lev, "Holy War Without End," *Chicago Tribune*, November 24, 1996.

———, "Tyranny of Religion Imperils Rich Culture," *Chicago Tribune*, December 3, 1996.

Timothy Maier, "Horror Stories," *Insight on the News*, May 13, 2003.

Middle East, "Doctor Reveals Mass Slaughter at Saddam's Largest Jail," August 2, 2001.

———, "Syria: Time to Break with Legacy of Torture and Dehumanization," September 19, 2001.

Emad Mekay, "An Economic Essential?" *Middle East*, November 1997.

Monitoring Media, "Iran: Journalist Given One Year Suspended Sentence," December 8, 2003.

Dave Montgomery, "Satellite Television Brings Outside World to Saudi Arabia," Knight Ridder/Tribune News Service, December 13, 2003.

John Murphy, "For Afghan Refugees, Childhood Is Labor," *Baltimore Sun*, October 21, 2003.

Raid Qusti, "Our 'Female Problem,'" *Washington Post*, July 9, 2002.

Fary Rosenblatt, "Between the Lines," *New York Jewish Week*, August 1, 2003.

Lara Sukhtian, "West Bank Town's Plight Highlights Barrier's Impact," *Columbian*, March 2, 2004.

Sunday Mirror (London), "The West at War," September 30, 2001.

Time, "About Face," December 3, 2001.

———, "The Women of Islam," December 3, 2001.

Time International, "The Child Soldiers," November 12, 2001.

Yaroslav Trofimov, "Saudi Shiites See Gains from U.S. Invasion of Iraq," *Wall Street Journal*, February 3, 2003.

Vivienne Walt, "Iraqi Children Working to Survive with Their Parents Struggling," *Boston Globe*, August 12, 2003.

Lawrence Wright, "Kingdom of Silence," *New Yorker*, January 5, 2004.

Internet Sources

Maya Alleruzzo, "Why Palestinian Children Die," Betar-Tagar UK, July 30, 2003. www.betar.co.uk/articles/betar1059578683.php.

Amnesty International, "Saudi Arabia Remains Fertile Ground for Torture with Impunity," May 2002. www.amnesty.org/library/index/ENGMDE2230042002.htm.

Amnesty International Canada, "Saudi Arabia: End Secrecy, End Suffering," 2000. www.amnesty.ca/SaudiArabia/1htm.

BBC News, "Campaigners Demand U.S. Torture Probe," December 27, 2002. http://news.bbc.co.uk/s/hi/americas/2607629.stm.

BBC World News, "World Court Examines Barrier Row," February 23, 2004. www.bbc.co.uk/2/hi/middle-east/3512255.stm.

Jeremy Cooke, "School Trains Suicide Bombers," *BBC News*, July 18, 2001.

http://news.bbc.co.uk/1/hi/world/middle_east/1446003.stm.

Borzou Daragahi, "I Would Build Skyscrapers. I Have Real Dreams!" *Arizona Daily Star*, March 19, 2004. www.dailystar.com.

———, "Kurds Say They Deserve More Rights, Land, Autonomy," *Washington Times*, March 15, 2004. www.washingtontimes.com/world/20040315-100009-9985r.htm.

Ken Ellingwood, "Fence Alters Life for Arabs," *Detroit News*, February 23, 2004. www.detnews.com/2004/nation/0402/23/a04_71662.htm.

Richard Engel, "Fundamentalists Demand Mafia-Style Protection Money from Copts," *Middle East Times*, April 1997. www.metimes.com/cens/gizia.htm.

Sajida Hayat, "Kabul: The City Where Even the Sunrise and Sunset Have Been Upset for a Long Time," Revolutionary Association of the Women of Afghanistan, January 2000. www.rawa.org/sajida.html.

Human Rights Watch, "The Internet in the Mideast and North Africa: Iraq," June 1999. www.hrw.org/advocacy/internet/mena/iraq.htm.

———, "The Internet in the Mideast and North Africa: Saudi Arabia," June 1999. www.hrw.org/advocacy/internet/mena/saudi.htm.

———, "The Internet in the Mideast and North Africa: Syria," June 1999. www.hrw.org/advocacy/internet/mena/syria.htm.

———, "Saudi Arabia: Religious Police Role in School Fire Criticized,"

March 15, 2002. www.hrw.org/press/ 2002/03/saudischool.htm.

Human Rights Watch World Report 2003, "Iran," www.hrw.org/wr2k3/mideast3. html.

Kurdistan Observer, "Kurds Protest Outside Syrian Parliament Against Discrimination," December 10, 2002. www.konews/11-12-02-kurds-pro test-outside-syrian-parli.htm.

Christina Lamb, "Taliban Brings Terror to Refugee Camps," *London Telegraph*, September 30, 2001. www.tele graph.co.uk.

Azadeh Moaveni, "The Age of Googoosh," *Time Europe*, August 28, 2000. www.time.com/time/europe/ webonly/mideast/2000/08/goo goosh.html.

Reporters Without Borders, "Censorship and Self-Censorship," April 2002. www.rsf.org/print.php3?id-article=1436.

———, "Regime Jails Journalist for Eight Years and Suspends More Publica-

tions," July 2002. www.rsf.org/print. php3?id-article=2075.

Susan Sachs, "Project: Open Book— Saudi Arabia," March 28, 2000. www.domini.org/openbook/sau20000 328.html.

John Sifton, "A Last Road Trip Through Premodern Afghanistan," Peace Pledge Union, September 30, 2001. www.ppu.org.uk/temp/last-trip.html.

Jonathan Silvers, "Child Labor in Pakistan," *Atlantic Monthly*, February 1996. www.theatlantic.com/issues/ 96feb/pakistan/pakistan.htm.

U.S. Copts Home Page, "Killing of Samir Wassef," June 1997. pweb.net-com.com/~us_copts/news.htm.

———, "Three Slain After Egypt Church Massacre," February 1997. pweb.net-com.com/~us_copts/news.htm

Vincent Vulin, "After Saddam, Shiites in Kuwait Becoming Vocal About Rights," *Gulf News Online*, March 12, 2004. www.gulf-news.com/Articles/ news.asp?ArticleID=113538.

INDEX

dancing, outlawing, 52

Dawa Party, 83

death penalty, 21–22

dress code, for women, 29–30, 37

Ebadi, Shirin, 42–43

education
of Afghani women, 30
child labor vs., 61–62
children's lack of, 64–65
of Saudi women, 34, 39

Egypt
artistic expression in, 49–51
child labor in, 61–64

employment
child labor and, 61–70
by women, 30–31, 34–35

Engel, Richard, 79

executions, in Iraq, 23–25, 85

films, banning of, 52–54

Gaza Strip, 74

gizia, 76, 77

Googoosh (Iranian singer), 52, 53

government, criticism of, 44–48

Hajizadeh, Moham-mad, 17

Hazaras, 81–82

health care, for women, 31–32

human rights, need for improving con-ditions for, 91

Human Rights Watch, 10, 26

Human Rights Watch World Report 2003, 17

Hussein, Saddam
artistic expression under, 48–49, 51
democratic execu-tions under, 23–25
persecution and vio-lence against Shi-ites under, 82–85
torture under, 22–23
treatment of Kurds under, 85–86

Intermediate School No. 31 fire (2002), 37–38

Internet, 57–59

Iran
artistic expression in, 51–54
censoring of theater in, 51–52
human rights abuses in
under Khomeini, 14–15
under shah, 13
imprisonment of journalists in, 45–47
justice system in, 15–17
possibility of change in, 17–18
sharia law in, 13–14
women's rights in, 41–43

Iraq
executions in, 23–25
Internet access in, 58
see also Hussein, Saddam

Internet access in, 58

lashes given to prisoners in, 18–20

needed reform for women in, 39

restrictions on journalists in, 47–48

torture of criminal suspects in, 18

treatment of women in, 34–37

Schulz, William F., 18

separate-but-not-equal rule, for women, 34–35, 37

sexual abuse, by U.S. soldiers, 27

sharia (Islamic law), 13–14, 16

Shiites

Iraq's violence and persecution against, 82–85

Saudi discrimination against, 79, 81

Taliban violence against, 81–82

Shobokshi, Hussein, 48

Silvers, Jonathan, 65, 66

Snowman, The (film), 52–54

Starbucks, 57

suicide bombings, 72, 74–75, 83

Sunnis, Shiites vs., 78–79

Syria

abuse of prisoners in, 16

discrimination against Kurds in, 86–89

Internet access in, 58–59

Tadmur prison (Syria), 16

Taliban

artistic expression under, 54–56

children used as soldiers by, 72

treatment of women under, 29–32

use of amputation for punishment by, 19

violence against Shiites by, 81–82

warlords challenged by, 28–29

television access, 59–60

torture

confessions and, 16–17, 18

interrogation of Taliban prisoners and, 25–26

under Hussein, 22–23

in Saudi Arabia, 18

in Tadmur prison, 16

United States, abuse of Middle East prisoners and, 25–27

Universal Declaration of Human Rights, 10, 12

visual arts

Saudi Arabia's laws on, 57

Taliban's prohibition of, 55–56

Wahhabism, 79, 81

war, human rights and, 25

West Bank, 89–90

PICTURE CREDITS

ABOUT THE AUTHOR

Gail B. Stewart received her undergraduate degree from Gustavus Adolphus College in St. Peter, Minnesota. She did her graduate work in English, linguistics, and curriculum study at the College of St. Thomas and the University of Minnesota. She taught English and reading for more than ten years.

She has written over ninety books for young people, including a series for Lucent Books called The Other America. She has written many books on historical topics such as World War I and the Warsaw ghetto.

Stewart and her husband live in Minneapolis with their three sons, Ted, Elliot, and Flynn; two dogs; and a cat. When she is not writing, she enjoys reading, walking, and watching her sons play soccer.